College Admission 101

Simple Answers To Tough Questions About College Admissions and Financial Aid

By Robert Franek
America's Leading College Expert from The Princeton Review

PrincetonReview.com

Penguin
Random
House

The Princeton Review
110 East 42nd St, 7th Floor
New York, NY 10017
editorialsupport@review.com

ISBN: 978-1-5247-5853-0
eBook ISBN: 978-1-5247-5854-7
ISSN: 2575-6273

The Princeton Review is not affiliated
with Princeton University.

Production: Best Content Solutions
Production Editor: Melissa Duclos

Printed in the United States of
America.

9 8 7 6 5 4 3 2

Editorial
Robert Franek, Editor-in-Chief
David Soto, Director of Content
Development
Steven Koch, Student Survey
Manager
Pia Aliperti, Senior Editor
Danielle Correa, Editor

**Penguin Random House Publishing
Team**
Tom Russell, VP, Publisher
Alison Stoltzfus, Publishing Director
Ellen L. Reed, Production Manager
Amanda Yee, Associate Managing
Editor
Suzanne Lee, Designer

Acknowledgments

This book would not have been possible without the following individuals at The Princeton Review and beyond: Kristen O'Toole, who was instrumental in the development of this title, and editors Pia Aliperti and Danielle Correa, Scott Harris of Best Content Solutions, and production editor Melissa Duclos, who transformed the various pieces of the manuscript into the book now in your hands. My continued thanks to our data collection masters David Soto and Stephen Koch for their successful efforts in collecting and accurately representing the statistical data that informs parts of this book.

Most of all, thank you to my readers—I hope this book proves useful in your college searches, applications, and overall college admission journeys. Keep asking the tough questions. Good luck!

Robert Franek

Table of Contents

Hands down, what I love best about my job here at The Princeton Review is spending direct, quality time with college-bound students and their families. It sounds like a canned talking point, right? The head of content for a global educational services company likes working with students and their families? But, I'm not fibbing, not even a syllable. Here's why—every day you teach me how to be better at my job.

I spend most of the academic year on the road speaking to students, parents, counselors, and educators alike. Whether I'm teaching students and parents the basics or the more advanced lessons around the college process, the most motivating part of that exchange is always the privilege of listening to each of you. Here's the logic: if I can understand your college goals along with the stuff that stresses you, confuses you, and plain-old scares you about the admissions process, then I can create the right kinds of resources to put you on the path to achieving those goals. Meeting and talking with you only reinforces my overall mission to assuage anxiety around the college admission process and create the next class of informed and fearless college shoppers. Now, that's awesome, indeed!

Corralled in this book are sixty of the savviest, college-related questions that you've asked me over the last two years. (I've reached nearly 50,000 people in live presentations this year alone and millions more on TV, radio, and online: this book is a testament that my ears have been listening on all fronts!) As the title of this book notes, these are tough questions. Important ones? Absolutely. My answers are direct and, yes, made simple. That doesn't mean the answers are dumbed down in any way. Here you'll find clear answers brought into sharp focus with actionable next steps.

Wondering how to start your college search? Which standardized tests to take? Have nitty-gritty questions about your high school schedule? How about the financial aid process? I've got you covered for each of these key questions, and so many more. My goal, and ours at The Princeton Review, is to help you succeed in each step of your educational journey. Consider *College Admission 101* your primer to do just that.

This book is for students in high school, parents of high schoolers (and even middle schoolers), parents who attended college themselves, parents who didn't attend college, families new to the United States, and more. In short, no one should ever feel excluded or unprepared for the college search and application process. From SAT scores to scholarships, this book casts a very wide net in answering questions about college topics and is meant for anyone and everyone interested in attending college.

Thanks to each of you for putting your faith in me and our full team at The Princeton Review. I very much hope you find this book a great resource in your college search. It's been a genuine pleasure bringing it to you.

Robert Franek

Introduction

The aim of this book is to address strategic college admission questions—the nitty-gritty application details that high school students and parents ask me about when I speak at college-bound events and webinars, and that The Princeton Review's own college admission experts hear from clients.

Before I get into the specifics of the college admission process, however, I want to address two larger questions that tend to appear on op-ed pages each fall:

Is a college degree worth the cost of tuition?

The cost of a four-year degree has been increasing faster than inflation for over 30 years. Ninety-eight percent of participants in our 2017 "College Hopes and Worries" survey reported that financial aid will be necessary to pay for college in 2017. At many institutions, financial aid includes loans, and so graduates often enter an uncertain job market already loaded with debt. With that in mind, is college really the path to professional success and financial stability?

My answer is an emphatic "yes!" Of course, I'm biased—I've worked in and around college admissions for over 20 years. I have seen first-hand how young people use the tools and experiences they acquire in colleges and universities to achieve their personal and professional goals. Fortunately, there are plenty of data to confirm my anecdotal observations:

In 2015, adults with bachelor's degrees saw significantly higher median earnings and a lower unemployment rate than those with only a high school diploma.

Education attained	2015 Unemployment rate	2015 Median weekly earnings
Bachelor's degree	2.8%	$1,137
High school diploma only	5.4%	$678
All workers	4.3%	$860

Note: Data are for persons age 25 and over. Earnings are for full-time wage and salary workers. Source: U.S. Bureau of Labor Statistics

According to a 2015 study by the University of Maine, workers with a college education are more likely to:

- Take advantage of a pension plan offered by their employers;

- Receive health insurance through their employers;

- Report having a strong understanding of political issues;

- Donate their time through volunteer activities.

These are merely the quantifiable gains—you'll have many, many valuable experiences on campus or as a direct result of your college experience. (I wrote about such experiences in another book, *Colleges That Create Futures: 50 Schools That Launch Careers By Going Beyond the Classroom.*)

If you, like me, accept the premise that a college degree is most definitely worth the cost of tuition, then that brings us to the other big question that so many students, parents, and media commentators grapple with.

What is the "best" college?

There isn't one.

It might seem silly to start this book with a question that has no answer, but this is an important point that will help put your whole college admission journey into perspective. I understand why folks ask: Given the awesome lifetime benefits we know a student can obtain with a college degree, it's common to make a correlative leap: the more prestigious the alma mater, the greater the rewards for the graduate. Planning, applying, and paying for college is an arduous and anxiety-inducing process, and students and their supporters want to be sure their hard work will pay off with a degree and experience that pave the way to a successful career. The data point that often demonstrates prestige or reputation—that is often a major factor in college ranking methodologies—is a college or university's selectivity.

According to our annual College Hopes and Worries survey, Stanford University has been the #1 Dream School for college-bound students and their parents for several years running. Stanford enjoys an excellent reputation, provides world-class resources, and features an impressive roster of alumni. We don't need to rely on our survey results to know it's a highly desirable school—last year nearly 44,000 students applied for admission. Stanford accepted just 5 percent of the applicant pool. Are the roughly 41,800 students who applied to Stanford and did not get in doomed to failure?

Of course not! And therein lies the fatal flaw in the myth of "the best college": There may not be a single best overall college, but there are absolutely schools that are the best for each and every one of those applicants, and a best school for you.

First, this assumption fuels an enormous amount of anxiety for college-bound students and their parents by creating the impression that the choices they make in high school determine, or limit, their future opportunities. You do not have to attend a highly selective school in order to pursue a meaningful and lucrative career.

School	Grads median starting salary*	Grads median mid-career salary*	% grads reporting high job meaning*	% applicants accepted**
Massachusetts Institute of Technology	$78,300	$134,000	62%	8%
State University of New York—Maritime College	$69,700	$144,000	58%	68%
Wittenberg University	$44,500	$94,900	69%	77%
University of North Dakota	$48,400	$81,700	68%	82%
Santa Clara University	$61,900	$121,000	49%	49%

*Data from PayScale.com College Salary Report 2016-17

**Data reported to The Princeton Review by the school in spring 2016

Planning, applying, and paying for college is an arduous and anxiety-inducing process, and students and their supporters want to be sure their hard work will pay off with a degree and experience that pave the way to a successful career. But after twenty years in this business, I can assure you that college and career prep are not one-size-fits-all—there are close to 4,000 four-year colleges in the United States. Thoughtful research and reflection will help you find the schools that fit you best.

Applying to schools that line up with your goals and interests also helps your chances of gaining acceptance. You will likely be asked why you want to attend a particular school in a supplemental essay or interview, and "Because you're the best!" won't cut it. If you identify the specific opportunities on campus that are exciting to you, that enthusiasm will come through on your application. Admissions officers are looking for students who will be active participants in their college community.

Now that we've dispensed with the "best college" myth, I have plenty to share with you about how to set yourself up for success in high school, maximize your SAT and ACT scores, find the colleges and universities that will fit you best, and craft competitive applications.

Survey Says

What's the biggest benefit of college?

42% say the potentially better job and higher income

32% say the exposure to new ideas

26% say the education

*Results of The Princeton Review's 2017 College Hopes & Worries Survey of college applicants and parents of college applicants.

Chapter 1

College Research

CHAPTER 1
College Research

The most common word you'll hear me say when advising students and parents on the college selection process is "fit." No two students are exactly alike, and no two colleges are exactly alike either. Any college can be a dream school for the right student, and any student can find a college that will give them a terrific education and college experience.

There are many factors you can consider when drafting a list of potential schools, and sometimes the factors that seem most important to families when starting out can be the least important in terms of a student's life on campus or their life after graduation. With this in mind, here's how and when to kick off your college search.

What criteria should I use to find a college or university where I can succeed?

When I give talks on college admissions around the country, I break "best fit" into three categories:
- Academic fit
- Cultural fit
- Financial fit
- Career fit

Your Best Academic Fit

This is probably the biggest of the four best-fit buckets. First and foremost, you want a school that offers the major(s) and classes that interest you. Many students have an idea of their major when they begin researching colleges, and a list of schools with strong departments in your field of choice is a great place to begin the college research process. If you're unsure of your future academic track, don't fret—you don't need to map out your entire career in your junior year in high school in order to find your best-fit colleges and universities. Read up on course descriptions and professor bios and look for topics and experiences that inspire you. Enthusiasm is key for getting the most out of your academic experience.

> Choosing a college where the courses on offer match your learning style will set you up to succeed.

Classroom format is just as important to keep in mind as content. Academics at liberal arts colleges that matriculate Bachelor of Art or Bachelor of Science degrees are often based on professor-student discussion in seminar-style classes. Larger institutions that offer a broad range of degrees and departments are likely to offer liberal arts style courses as well as larger formats: lectures, labs, and breakout sessions with teaching assistants (typically graduate students). Choosing a college where the courses on offer match your learning style will set you up to succeed. To the same point, look for academic support resources you might need: most campuses have writing centers (often dedicated specifically to first year students in required college writing courses) and peer-to-peer tutoring available to all students. If you plan to formally apply for support services, be sure to contact the academic support center on campus to review requirements, the approval process, and available resources. (You can learn more about specific services and applying for academic support in *The K&W Guide to Colleges for Students with Learning Differences* by my friends Marybeth Kravets and Imy Wax.)

Not all academic opportunities happen in the classroom, either: go beyond department descriptions to look at any dedicated resources, opportunities to travel here or abroad, or experiential learning centers on campus (and make sure they're available to undergraduates!).

- Students at University of Alabama's College of Communication and Information Science can gain valuable professional experience at their Digital Media Center.
- In Maine, Bowdoin College owns several acres on a nearby island, home to the Schiller Coastal Studies Center, providing hands-on research tools for environmental studies and biology students.
- At Babson College in Wellesley, Massachusetts, the Center for Women's Entrepreneurial Leadership is available to undergraduate students through the CWEL Scholars program. CWEL Scholars work with "near-peer" mentors and gain professional competencies like presentation and negotiation skills.

> Go beyond the classroom to look at travel, research, and experiential learning opportunities.

These are just three examples—each of these schools offers tons of other opportunities, and every college and university in the country has unique resources and programs.

Does all of the above sound aggressively aspirational? Good. Aspiration is the secret sauce that helps you stay motivated and engaged through the long college application process, and can help shine a spotlight on your application for admission officers. Ultimately, though, academic fit isn't based solely on aspirations: eventually, you will need to look at the application data each university releases annually and compare it to your own stats. If your GPA and standardized test scores fall short of the averages of the current first year class at your dream school, there are two important steps to take:

1. Expand your school list. Even if you have your heart set on a particular institution, I guarantee there is another one where you will be successful and satisfied. You can keep your eyes on your prize school while ensuring that you have more than one back up plan.

2. Make a plan to improve your grades and/or your test scores. This will be tailored to the improvements you want to make and how much time you have to make them before submitting college applications in the fall and winter of your senior year of high school. Chapters 2 and 3 of this book cover standardized tests and high school classes and grades in detail.

Your Best Cultural Fit

"Cultural fit" can be tough to define. In this category, I include some concrete aspects of college life: institution size, demographics, location (and weather, believe it or not), dorms, dining services, extracurricular facilities (like the campus gym or theater) and activities (like clubs, sports, or Greek life), and campus speakers and events. But this category can also include elements that are harder to quantify: how do you feel when you're on campus, or checking out the college community online? You don't have to make a vision board of your college life, but you want to be able to picture yourself feeling comfortable on campus.

Start with practical matters: size and location. When I refer to campus size, I'm talking about the student population, not the acreage. The number of students on campus and the percentage of those students who will be your cohort—for example, at a college of liberal arts or engineering within a research university—will influence your day-to-day experience. It's also relevant to student/faculty ratio and class size, which I referenced above in relation to learning style. Typically schools with low student/faculty ratios see more interaction between those populations, which can allow for additional academic support during office hours and valuable mentor or professional networking relationships. If you're considering

> You don't have to make a vision board of your college life, but you want to be able to picture yourself feeling comfortable on campus.

larger schools, be sure to ask about registration and accessibility—is it easy to get the classes you want on your schedule, or competitive? This is a great question for current students—I don't recommend harassing strangers, but you will likely meet student representatives when you visit campus (I'll cover more about campus visits later in this chapter), and you can ask the admission office if they have a list of students who have volunteered to answer questions for prospective applicants.

The size of your university will also impact town-gown relations, or the overall relationship between the institution and the surrounding community, which includes your prospects for internships, part-time work, and off-campus activities. There are towns that primarily revolve around the large universities therein, like Ann Arbor, Michigan, or Clemson, South Carolina, and there are small, rural campuses that offer a more contained experience (which students often describe as a "bubble," with both positive and negative connotations), like Colby College in Maine or Oberlin College in Ohio. Going to college in a large city where the university is just one of many influences and employers, like Philadelphia or Chicago, is a very different experience that might come with more distractions as well as a wide range of off-campus professional opportunities. You probably already have some idea about whether you'd prefer a rural or suburban campus, or how far from home you'd like to be. Use your campus visits to refine those preferences: what does one experience offer that the other does not? Which more closely aligns with your goals? Whether you want to go to college close to where you grew up or across the country, you will need to factor travel and/or commuting costs into your college financial planning.

Beyond these basics, think about how you want to spend your time outside of class, and look for indicators of campus social life. Do students stay on campus during the weekends? What kind of social events does the school host? Which clubs are the most popular? Does student social life revolve around Saturday football games or quiet get-togethers, or a combination of both? If the school has fraternities and sororities, what percentage of the population goes Greek? These are just a few questions that can help you begin to identify what you want in a school and how to look for it. If you want to pursue any specific extracurricular activities in college, whether they made your high school resume or you want to find new opportunities, that's a great place to start: Look for clubs or facilities dedicated to those activities and find out what you can about how accessible they are and if there's a campus community dedicated to what you're interested in. You might even find a club you want to start on campus—if that's the case, ask about the process for setting up a club charter and available school funding for student groups. This is often the most fun part of college research.

The physical layout of a campus can also tell you a lot about how and where students socialize. First year students living on campus are often housed together and organized into smaller groups under resident advisors (RAs). RAs are there to help facilitate com-

> If you absolutely can't get to campus, social media is your friend.

munal living and maintenance of shared spaces, but may also be responsible for dorm parties and other activities that foster interaction and community-building. Outside the dorms, where do students spend time? In the library or the gym? On the quad or in the coffeehouse? All of the above? A single dining hall on campus can build a sense of unity within the student body, but it might be overwhelming for some introverted students. (Don't forget to ask about dining services, especially if you have any dietary restrictions. You'll be eating this food for four years, after all.) If most students live off campus after their first year, are there student-friendly neighborhoods and businesses close to campus? One of my favorite things to do when I visit a new campus is people-watch in between classes. When the bell rings, you'll see an amazing cross section of students moving from one class to the next, and likely get a sense of where students gather when they're just hanging out. If you're only on campus for a short time, this is an awesome way to form a loose impression of the student body. I am a big advocate for campus visits (more on that at the end of this chapter), but if you absolutely can't get to campus, social media is your friend. Go beyond the official school accounts and check out any school spirit hashtags, or geo-tags on campus—that way you'll see real-life posts from real students.

It's impossible to quantify every aspect of a campus social scene, and the best way to observe it is up close. Many schools offer applicants the option to stay with first or second year students in a dorm for the night and see what campus life is really like. You don't have to do this for every school where you plan to apply, but if possible, give it a go at your top choice schools. Because these visits are arranged through the admissions office, they are also a means of indicating your interest in the school to admissions officers. If interviews are a part of the admissions process and are available on campus, schedule yours the day after your overnight visit. Your impressions of the campus will be fresh, so the interviewer will gain insight into what excites you about the school, and spending time on campus will give you a chance to think about what you need to know about the school to be sure it's the best fit for you. Interviewers love good questions as much as good answers.

Your Best Financial Fit

Financial fit boils down to: Can you afford to attend this school?

I never tell students to cross a school off their list solely because it's too expensive—there is a lot of financial aid out there ($181 billion total aid was available in 2017, according to The College Board's "Trends in Student Aid" report) and many different paths to pay for college. But when it comes time to commit to a college in the spring of your senior year of high school, it's important to consider cost. So keep that pricey private school on your list, but apply to a "financial safety school," too. That's a college or university that fits you academically and culturally and that you know you can afford—look at public universities, where tuition is cheaper for state residents. Other options here include living at home or with relatives while attending school, saving the cost of room and board, or attending a community college for a year or two and then transferring to your dream university for a degree. The latter is a very affordable path to a college degree, but bear in mind that you will need to maintain stellar grades in order to be accepted as a transfer student at a competitive institution.

Parents, you will most likely bear most of the responsibility for defining "financial fit" for your student. It is very important to take a hard look at your finances, make a budget covering the tuition you can afford, and review financial aid options. I cover this in more detail in Chapter 5, and you can find detailed strategies for saving money and completing necessary forms in our book *Paying for College Without Going Broke* by my friend Kal Chany. Every school that receives federal aid is required to offer students a "calculator" that will help them project the financial aid they will receive (although keep in mind that these calculators are rarely exact). As I noted in my introduction, many aid packages include loans, and you can look up the average debt carried by recent graduates of every institution for a ballpark estimate on what your student will be carrying when they enter the job market. Some selective institutions advertise that their policy allows them to meet demonstrated student need entirely without loans—if that is the primary reason you are interested in an institution, contact the financial aid office for details early on in your application process. Even with such policies, not every student will graduate debt-free.

Your Best Career Fit

In addition to making sure the schools you're considering offer the majors and classes that interest you, I also recommend visiting or contacting the career development center at each. Find out how the school supports students in preparing for the professional world: do they offer resume writing workshops? Practice interviews? Networking events with alumni? If you foresee yourself in a particular field, location, or specific workplace, ask about past students' track records of finding internships and entry-level jobs in those areas. College admission officers and career counselors are happy to highlight their institutions' success stories! If you're not sure yet which direction you'll go in, see if career coaching and personal evaluations are available for students. Many institutions extend career support to alumni, too, which can be invaluable in the early post-collegiate years. As more and more students are factoring post-graduate plans into their college decision process, college admission and recruitment officers emphasize career support and placement when pitching their schools to prospective applicants.

Survey Says

Ideally, how far from home would you like college to be?

Parents: 50% say fewer than 250 miles from home

Students: 68% say more than 250 miles from home

*Results of The Princeton Review's 2017 College Hopes & Worries Survey of college applicants and parents of college applicants.

How important are college rankings?

On the one hand, I kicked off this book by telling you there's no one best college to rule them all, so you might be expecting me to say college rankings aren't very important. On the other hand, I also publish an annual *Best Colleges* book full of college ranking lists. In the words of Walt Whitman, "Do I contradict myself? Very well then I contradict myself, (I am large, I contain multitudes.)"

> It's important to understand the methodology behind any college ranking list you're using to fully understand what the ranking is telling you about the school.

There are a lot of different college ranking lists available. Think of these as tools to help you find your best-fit school. A list that claims to rank schools overall is not a very precise tool. These lists are often based on the GPA and standardized test scores of enrolled students and on the school's acceptance rate. That doesn't make the #1 ranked college the best college, it makes it the most competitive. And rankings that include things like "reputation" or "prestige" typically define those as the opinions of academics or other college presidents, not employers or hiring managers or even current students. It's important to understand the methodology behind any ranking list you're using to fully understand what the ranking is telling you about the school. "Best value" college lists are typically based on college costs, financial aid packages, and graduate debt, and thus are perhaps more informative than ranking lists based on selectivity and reputation. If you're looking at a "best value" college ranking list, check the methodology for data points that underscore student success: retention (i.e., the percentage of students that return for sophomore year), 4-year graduation rate, and data that points to career placement or starting salary. These factors really do add up to a meaningful measurement of value.

Narrowly-defined college ranking lists in specific categories that reflect what is important to you can really help you identify your best fit schools. The Princeton Review publishes over sixty undergraduate lists annually, most of which are based on surveys of current students—the only experts on what life is like on their campuses. We survey tens of thousands of students annually to be sure we have an accurate, up-to-date picture of life on campus. We ask students how many hours they study outside of class each week, what they think of their school administration, career services, research opportunities, study abroad programs, campus newspaper, college town, and tons more. We ask about dorms, food, political leanings, and even how happy students are (though the latter occasionally inspires some existential rumination in our open ended answers). We know which school has the top-rated radio station and theater productions, and even how much students are drinking on campus. Every year I get a few calls from administrators who are worried about where their schools landed on the rankings, but my goal is to provide information provided by real students to real applicants. You need a full and honest picture of campus life to find the schools that will best fit your goals, your learning style, and your personality.

Campus Visit Advice from a Student Who Has Been There

"Visit! The feel of a school is entirely important. I visited what I thought would be my top school and campus didn't feel like home. On the other hand, I visited a college I didn't think I would be interested in and it just felt right."

—2017 College Hopes & Worries Survey

When should I start my college research?

You will want to have your final list of colleges by early fall senior year. Making that list will require a lot of research and synthesizing information, so it's a good idea to start browsing colleges in 10th grade. Start by making a list of every college that appeals to you, and then get to work learning about each one. You may end up crossing some off quickly if they're too far from home (or too near), don't have a team that competes in your sport, or don't graduate many students in your field of interest. This early research phase will help you define your best fit school criteria, as well. As you shape your list, look for common elements among the schools that interest you, and seek out other colleges and universities that share those qualities. If there's a college counselor at your school, ask for a meeting to discuss your interests. Your college counselor may be able to recommend schools for your list, and help identify additional support you may need to get into college, like an academic tutor, standardized test prep, or a private college coach. (Even if your counselor is not available to you until the 11th grade, starting your research early will help you find any gaps in your academic and admissions resources.) If you have a list of twenty possible schools where you'd consider applying at the end of 10th grade, you're well on your way to finding the college that fits you best. You may have a much shorter list if you had a clear idea of your "best fit" when you began your search, but there's no need to limit your options yet.

> Visiting at least a few colleges will really help you get a sense of what you can expect and where you'll be happy.

During your junior year, your top priorities should be earning stellar grades and nailing your standardized tests (Chapter 2 covers the SAT and ACT in full), but you'll need to refine that list a little. This is a good time to reach out to any current students you know, and to begin visiting campuses if possible. If there is a college fair in your area, or college reps visit your high school, take the time to meet with them. You'll learn more about how each college markets itself, and be able to signal your interest to schools. By the end of junior year, you will want to have a clear idea where you want to go, what "best fit" means to you, and whether your grades and test scores are competitive for the schools on your list.

How many schools should I apply to?

I recommend choosing six schools:
- Two dream schools (or "reach" schools)
- Two match schools (where you'll probably, but not necessarily, be accepted)
- Two safety schools (you and your counselor are very confident you'll be accepted, and be able to afford tuition)

You can adjust this number up or down as needed, but you should apply to at least one school in each category, and you don't need to apply to ten or more schools.

A Crash Course in College Research

These seven sources of information have become staples for most college-bound students in their search for the right institution:

1. **College admission websites, brochures, videos, and catalogs.** You'll get a good idea of a school's academic offerings and admissions requirements.
2. **Current students.** No one knows schools better than the students who attend them.
3. **College Guides.** The Princeton Review's own *Best Colleges* is a great narrative guide based on real student quotes about their colleges.
4. **College profiles.** The Princeton Review's college search offers useful information about tuition, financial aid, and more while helping students like you find and compare schools, based on specific criteria.
5. **College rankings.** Our college ranking lists cover a range of topics that applicants might be curious about such as academics, financial aid, campus amenities, and much more.
6. **College forums/discussion boards.** Unfiltered feedback from all types of sources is exciting!
7. **Your college counselor.** They will help guide your overall college search and strategize for your best application when it comes time to apply.

Survey Says

How many colleges do students apply to?

42% said they (or their child) would apply to 5 to 8 colleges

30% said they (or their child) would apply to 9 or more colleges

*Results of The Princeton Review's 2017 College Hopes & Worries Survey of college applicants and parents of college applicants.

Is visiting campuses necessary?

Visiting the campuses of the colleges and universities where you are interested in studying is not required for admission (although a few schools, like Bard College, offer unique "Immediate Decision" application options in which you can get an admissions decision after visiting for a day, and submitting all your application materials, of course). Visiting at least a few colleges, however, will really help you get a sense of what you can expect and where you'll be happy.

School vacations are obviously a very convenient time to visit colleges, and I don't advocate skipping school days to check out colleges! But bear in mind that visiting an empty campus will make a very different impression than visiting a campus filled with students. You probably won't be able to visit every school on your list while classes are in session, so here are my three tips:

- If you can only visit one or two schools while students are on campus, make them the schools that excite you the most.
- Check the semester calendars on campus websites—if your spring break schedule is different than that of the college, students will be in class while you're free to visit.
- If you're planning to visit colleges over the summer, try to do so in late August—students will be trickling back, varsity athletes will be on campus for practice, and you may get to see some of the pre-orientation activities the school runs for first-year students.

Your campus visit will most likely include a tour led by a current student, in a group with other prospective applicants and their families. This is an awesome opportunity to get insight into daily life on campus, so do not hesitate to ask your tour guide for their opinion on any aspect of the college. Even if you're curious about a department or extracurricular activity the tour guide does not participate in, they may be able to share insights via roommates or friends. The other high school students in your tour group are also assets—listen to their questions and if you have time, ask about their experiences visiting other schools. How your tour guide answers questions will tell you much more about the school than the history and trivia they're likely reciting as they lead you around.

Depending on the time of year when you visit a college, there may be prospective student events available beyond the standard tour, like a question and answer session with deans or admission officers, also known as an information session. This is an opportunity to ask questions about financial aid, career services, academic support, curriculum requirements (many, though not all, schools have some general education requirements that all students must complete, regardless of major), and availability of classes, particularly for first years and/or prerequisites for more advanced courses.

> In most admissions cases, interviews are optional, and are available on campus, via alumni in your area, or on Skype.

If you are visiting a college where you know you plan to apply, try to schedule an interview while you are on campus. In most admissions cases, interviews are optional, and are available on campus, via alumni in your area, or on Skype. An on-campus interview with an admissions staffer is a great opportunity: (alumni interviewers are awesome and the admissions office will absolutely take their feedback seriously, but don't pass up an opportunity to connect with someone who has a hand in shepherding applications along). In your interview, you'll want to come off as articulate about and engaged with the things that are important to you, and have a clear idea of how this school above all others will help you pursue those passions. If you have this conversation when you've just toured campus and the school's unique features are fresh in your mind, it will be that much smoother. I cover interviews in much more detail in Chapter 6.

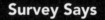

Survey Says

Which college are you (or your child) most likely to choose?

42% say college that will be the best overall fit

41% say college with the best program for my (my child's) career interests

9% say college with best academic reputation

8% say college that will be the most affordable

*Results of The Princeton Review's 2017 College Hopes & Worries Survey of college applicants and parents of college applicants.

What's an Information Session?

Here's what to expect

Colleges host information sessions led by admissions officers. Held on campus or locally when colleges visit high schools and college fairs, information sessions can be a great way to learn more about schools that interest you, or to find out about a school you're not yet familiar with.

Info sessions give a broad overview of the college—the size and geographic representation of the college, popular majors, the average class size, special academic programs, and activities many of their students take advantage of.

It's the presenter's job to get the audience interested in the school. So you'll also hear about any distinctions the college is proud of, like ranking lists they're featured on, the newly built energy efficient dorms, or how many Nobel Prize-winning professors are on campus.

While it's a good idea to bring any questions you have about the college, you're not likely to get answers to questions about your chances of admission, like, "Are my SAT scores high enough?" The presenter isn't in a position to evaluate your candidacy in that setting and will be hesitant to say anything that could later make you feel misled when you get your admissions decision.

Instead, ask questions about the admissions process and the typical student the college admits. That will allow the presenter to give you the information they're comfortable sharing, like whether or not interviews are offered, the ranges of GPAs and test scores for admits, and the importance the school places on essays and letters of recommendations.

Think of a college information session like a more personal version of a brochure. You may not be able to decide whether or not the college is right for you based on the session alone. You learn more, you get questions answered by a live human being and you get clues about whether or not you want to do even more research about the school.

10 College Opportunities That Go Beyond the Classroom

Cooperative Education	Students alternate paid professional experiences with coursework. They take classes for one semester, work full-time for one semester in their co-op, and repeat. **Real campus example:** Northeastern University puts students in 11,000 co-op placements last year!
Externship Programs	Externships are temporary job-shadowing programs that last anywhere from an afternoon to a few weeks. **Real campus example:** In the Spring Break Externship Program, Grinnell College matches first and second years with alumni as a way to help students explore a potential career.
Internship Programs	Many schools have programs that will fund unpaid or low-paying internships, which allow students to learn more about a field or organization of interest while completing tasks or projects alongside real employees. **Real campus example:** Every year, the 500 students in Vassar College's Field Work program lend their talents to nonprofits, government agencies, human services organizations, and businesses.

Leadership Training	Many colleges have dedicated leadership centers to train and mentor students in crucial skills like communication and teamwork. **Real campus example:** Undergrads at Gettysburg College can work with Leadership Coaches to apply for positions on campus and beyond. It's all part of the process to earn a Leadership Certificate from the Garthwait Leadership Center.
Projects	Projects are extended problem-solving activities that students can complete solo or in collaboration with a group, like composing a piece of music, writing a business plan, or designing a prototype. **Real campus example:** At Arizona State University, the Arts Venture Incubator helps students secure training, seed-funding, and one-on-one coaching to develop creative ventures for artists.
Research	On-campus research experiences can include working alongside your professor in a lab, writing a thesis, or completing a capstone project for your major. **Real campus example:** At Binghamton University, Summer Scholars and Artists Fellowships fund student research and creative projects during the summer.

Service Learning	Just like it sounds, service learning combines a learning experience with community service. Students develop a greater understanding of community issues and gain skills in critical-thinking and collaboration. **Real campus example:** Sharpe Community Scholars at William & Mary participate in local community projects that develop their problem-solving skills.
Student Organizations	Campus clubs bring together students with a common interest and help them have fun and develop leadership and teamwork experience. **Real campus example:** Students on the Alma College Model UN team debate current issues, earning valuable skills in public speaking and negotiation.
Unique Campus Facilities	Find the theater, lab, newsroom, or makerspace on campus that lets you build skills while doing something you love. **Real campus example:** Trinity University has professional radio and HD TV stations on campus where students produce their own content.

| Study Abroad | Colleges with robust study abroad programs help facilitate academic, internship, and cultural experiences outside of the United States.

Real campus example: Business and engineering sophomores in the University of Pittsburgh Plus3 Program can study the smartphone industry in China, car manufacturing in Germany, or coffee production in Costa Rica. |
| --- | --- |

Chapter 2

Standardized Tests

CHAPTER 2
Standardized Tests

SAT and ACT scores take the lead, but college admissions officers consider your performance on other standardized tests as well. High scores can even earn you scholarship dollars.

Students often ask me what tests they need to take and when. After all, there's the PSAT, AP exams, and SAT Subject Tests, oh my! Here's what I tell families about test scores and college admissions.

How are SAT or ACT scores used in the admission process and how important are they?

The SAT and ACT are standardized tests that are commonly used in the college admission process. The SAT is scored out of a total of 1600, and the ACT is scored out of a total of 36. The aim of both tests is to reflect students' preparedness and potential for academic success in college. Some states use either the SAT or ACT as a requirement for high school graduation. Most high school students will take one or both of these tests in 11th or 12th grade.

Why do admissions officers need a standardized test score alongside your high school grades? Because grading methodology differs from one high school to the next—standardized test scores put everyone on the same scale, at least in theory. This is very much a point of debate for those of us who follow college admission trends closely, and familiarity with test-taking techniques like pacing and guessing strategies can help students raise their scores—so the SAT and ACT may not be quite the objective measurements for success that the College Board and ACT, Inc. would have us believe. Regardless, they still present an important hurdle to clear in your race to a college degree, and The Princeton Review was founded to help students clear that hurdle with ease.

The importance of SAT or ACT scores in the college application process is different at each institution of higher education, and many liberal arts schools emphasize their holistic approach to application review, which means your application is read as a story about you rather than a lab report on your education. Earning high scores, however, remains a crucial part of your college admission process. There are still state university systems that have minimum score requirements, or offer guaranteed acceptance for in-state applicants with scores above a certain threshold. A low test score on an otherwise stellar application will raise red flags for readers, and these scores are often used to determine merit aid eligibility—merit aid will help you pay for college without taking on debt. No matter where you apply, the three most important elements of your college application will be your test scores, your GPA, and your high school transcript (i.e., the courses you choose to take—more on that in Chapter 3!).

Survey Says

What is the toughest part of the college admission process?

37% said taking SAT, ACT, or AP exams

33% said completing applications for admission and financial aid

21% said waiting for the decision letters; choosing which college to attend

9% said researching colleges; choosing schools to apply to

*Results of The Princeton Review's 2017 College Hopes & Worries Survey of college applicants and parents of college applicants.

Will colleges see my PSAT scores?

No, PSAT scores are not used in college admissions.

The PSAT is taken by roughly 1.4 million 11th graders each October. Your score will give you some idea of how you'll do on the SAT, which can help you form a clear plan to prep if you don't have one yet. But the PSAT isn't just a practice SAT—it will determine your eligibility for National Merit Scholarships, which can help you pay for college. So you should get

> The PSAT isn't just a practice SAT—it will determine your eligibility for National Merit Scholarships.

comfortable with the PSAT before you take it. I recommend preparing for all your standardized tests during the summer between 10th and 11th grade, before you've taken the PSAT. Why? First, prepping for the SAT and/or ACT in the summer will allow you to focus on your grades during the school year. Second, the best way to prepare for the PSAT is by preparing for the SAT itself. This will help you to use your PSAT score report to identify areas to focus on for the SAT, maximizing your study time. It will also increase your chances of scoring well enough to earn a National Merit Scholarship.

How is the PSAT used in determining National Merit Scholarships?

Students whose scores put them in the top 99th percentile of 11th grade PSAT takers for their state are recognized as National Merit Semifinalists. Historically, this percentile has included about 16,000 students. These top scorers are invited to submit their high school records, teacher recommendations, and a personal essay; many go on to win $2,500 merit scholarships while a lucky few are offered larger scholarships by colleges looking to attract students with high scores. Pretty good motivation to try a little practice for the PSAT! Another 34,000 or so students who score well on the test but do not make the 99th score percentile in their states receive official letters of recognition from the National Merit Scholarship Corporation. While official recognition won't help you pay for college, it will help highlight your application inside the admissions office—especially if you follow through and score well on the SAT or ACT.

Should I take the ACT or SAT?

I hear this question a lot! The vast majority of four-year colleges will accept scores from either test, and do not prefer one over the other, so it's really up to you. Most of the students we work with at The Princeton Review want guidance as to which test will allow them to get the highest score with the least amount of work. The simplest way to answer that question is to take a practice ACT and a practice SAT, including observing the standard time limits, and see how you feel and how you score. There are plenty of free or affordable ways to access practice tests online or in books.

The SAT was redesigned in 2016, so it's a different test than the one your parents remember taking. It's also more similar to the ACT than ever, which makes it much easier to prep for both tests concurrently. You don't have to take both the SAT and ACT, but a steadily increasing number of applicants to competitive colleges are submitting scores from both tests with their applications. That's definitely a trend to watch.

	SAT	**ACT**
Sections	Reading Writing & Language Math Essay (optional)	English Math Reading Science Reasoning Essay (Optional)

Time	3 hours (without Essay)
	3 hours 50 minutes
	  (with Essay)
		2 hours 55 minutes
		  (without Essay)
		3 hours 40 minutes
		  (with Essay)

Reading Comprehension	5 passages	4 passages
Science	None	1 "science" section that really tests critical thinking, not the science you learned in school
Math	Arithmetic Algebra I & II Geometry, Trigonometry, Data Analysis *Calculator not allowed on some sections	Arithmetic Algebra I & II Geometry, Trigonometry *Calculator allowed on all sections
Essay	Optional (but required by some colleges). The essay prompt is designed to test your comprehension of a source text.	Optional (but required by some colleges). The essay prompt is designed to test how well you evaluate and analyze complex issues.
Score	400-1600	1-36

The Scoop on Standardized Tests
(From Real Students Who Have Been There)

1. **On scheduling:** "Stagger your standardized tests—you don't want to be taking the APs at the same time as the SATs and SAT Subject Tests!"

2. **On getting a head start:** "Finish taking all standardized tests by junior year so in the fall of senior year, you can focus on your applications."

3. **On keeping your eye on the prize:** "If standardized testing like SATs or ACTs are required [by your colleges], start test prep early... to get in the most practice and confidence. But most importantly, keep in mind that this work will pay off!"

4. **On using breaks from school wisely:** "Start early and study for standardized tests over the summer."

5. **On choosing which tests to take:** "If your school offers them, take AP and Honors-level courses that align with your interests. By doing this, you can simultaneously explore and develop your passions while showing it to the colleges you apply to."

6. **On finding time to study:** "There needs to be a balance. Spending at least an hour a week prepping for the SAT/ACT will really help in the long run."

7. **On prepping to retake a test:** "Retake the SAT and/or ACT a couple times to improve scores and spend serious practice time between tests."

8. **On time management:** "When in doubt, dedicate a little time each day towards studying for the SAT/ACT, studying for AP exams, working on applications, and/or applying for scholarships. One piece of advice that I've heard and wholeheartedly agree with is that applying to college is basically like taking up a part-time job, in terms of both the time commitment and the effort you need to put in to be successful."

*Results of The Princeton Review's 2017 College Hopes & Worries Survey.

What does it mean when a college or university is "test optional"?

Real talk: you can get into college even if you bomb on your standardized tests. You can get into college without ever taking a standardized test, provided you have strong grades in challenging classes and apply to one of the nearly 1,000 accredited institutions that are test optional.

As I mentioned at the start of this chapter, whether standardized test scores truly help level the admissions playing field for students is debatable. Over the past dozen years, some colleges have tweaked their application processes to put less weight on SAT and ACT scores, or make submitting them entirely optional. This aligns with admissions policies that call for a holistic view of applications, and underscores the importance of best fit between student and school (because it tells us that schools are looking for something more than the highest grades and scores).

Often, applying without test scores requires submission of additional application materials, or meeting a specific GPA requirement. In other cases, you can apply for admission without test scores, but you'll still need to submit them to be considered for merit-based financial aid. You should research the admissions policies at your college of choice very carefully. FairTest.org is an excellent resource for students seeking more information about test-optional schools.

> I strongly recommend giving at least one test a try.

I strongly recommend giving at least one test a try, though. Having solid test scores on hand will give you a wider array of options when it comes to colleges, and may be necessary for scholarship applications.

When should I take the SAT or ACT?

Plan to take your first official sitting of either test in the spring of 11th grade. That will leave you with plenty of time to get your scores, and if you want to raise them, plan for any targeted follow-up prep and a second official sitting. If you're happy with your scores after the first test you take, great job! You could consider giving the other test a try, or just check scores off your list and use 12th grade fall to focus on crafting your applications and essays.

SAT and ACT Quick Calendar		
SAT*	7 times a year	August October November December March May June
ACT**	7 times a year	September October December February April June July

*Not all SAT Subject Tests are offered on each SAT test date.

**No test centers are scheduled in New York for the February and July ACT test dates. No test centers are scheduled in California for the July test date.

If I take either test more than once, which scores will colleges see?

Colleges and universities typically choose one of three options when it comes time to evaluate your standardized test scores:
- Consider all scores from all official test dates;
- Consider your highest overall score from a single test date;
- Consider a composite of your highest scores on each section from all the dates you took the test, or a "superscore."

Each school will have their policy clearly spelled out on the institution website and/or in your application materials. If you aren't sure which scores a school will evaluate with your application, call and ask. This will inform your test prep and test-taking strategy. It's also your responsibility to arrange to have the appropriate score reports sent to each college from ACT, Inc. or the College Board for the SAT. It's possible that you'll apply to several schools with different test score policies.

All Scores

If you're applying to any schools that require all your official score reports, you will want to be at the absolute top of your game each time you sit for either the SAT or ACT. Practice, practice, practice on full-length tests with the appropriate time limits as much as possible. Eliminate as many test-day variables as you possibly can: Make sure you know how to get to the test site in advance, have gas in the car and batteries in your calculator, get a good night's sleep and eat a healthy breakfast. I give this advice to all test takers, but if schools will see all your score reports, you can't afford any flubs. Fortunately, fewer and fewer schools are taking this intimidating approach to test scores, and if you do experience a standardized test tragedy, you can include a statement explaining the circumstances with your college application.

Highest Overall Score From a Single Test Date

Schools that only consider your highest overall score make the process of requesting score reports very simple, since you'll only need the one report.

Superscores

Many selective colleges use superscores, which is great for applicants: only your best test performances count on your application. You can calculate your SAT superscore by adding your highest Math section score to your highest Evidence-Based Reading and Writing score. You can calculate your ACT superscore by finding the average of your highest scores on Math, Science, Reading, and English sections. When you apply to a school with a superscore policy, you will need to identify the test dates on which you received your highest score on each test section (Math and Evidence-Based Reading and Writing on the SAT; Math, English, Reading, and Science on the ACT) and send in score reports from each of those dates. The admissions office will then calculate your superscore and dismiss the lesser scores.

The College Board and ACT, Inc. have historically charged a small fee for each score report. Colleges are increasingly accepting self-reported scores on applications—that means you won't have to pay for each official report to be sent to each school where you are applying, but can enter scores on your application yourself. You will still need to send in an official score report to confirm your self-reported scores if you are accepted. The College Board and ACT, Inc. have also introduced more fee-waiver policies that make it easier and cheaper for students to submit official score reports with their applications.

What are SAT Subject Tests? Which ones should I take, and when?

> Most schools will leave the subjects up to you, but sometimes admissions officers will want to see scores from specific tests, like Math Level 2.

SAT Subject Tests are one-hour multiple choice tests in specific academic subjects. They used to be called "SAT IIs" back when the main SAT was officially the "SAT I." Many selective colleges require or recommend that applicants submit scores from two to three SAT Subject Tests to be considered for admission. Most of these schools will leave the subjects up to you, but sometimes admission officers want to see scores from specific tests, like Math Level 2. If you don't have a list of schools where you'll be applying yet, you should plan to take at least two SAT Subject Tests in subjects that you enjoy and in which you earn good grades.

SAT Subject Tests are offered on SAT test dates, except for March, and not all subjects are available on every test date. You can take up to three SAT Subject Tests on a given test day, but you can't take the regular SAT and an SAT Subject Test on the same day (why you'd want to do such a thing, I can't imagine! You'll find my tips for staying sane through the college process in Chapter 8.) You will want to spread these tests out over your high school career rather than try to cram them all in junior year when you've started planning for college in earnest. It will also be easier to achieve a high score if you take an SAT Subject Test immediately after you complete the corresponding high school course. For example, if you take biology in 9th grade, take the SAT Subject Test in biology in May or June of 9th grade.

While SAT Subject Test scores do not carry as much weight as regular SAT scores on your college application, you still want to do well on these tests. You can prep with a book or a tutor, or talk to the teacher you have in a relevant subject—if enough students in your class are planning to take the SAT Subject Test in that subject, your teacher might be willing to lead a couple of extra study sessions outside of class ahead of the test date.

Do I need to take AP exams?

Most colleges and universities do not require Advanced Placement (AP) scores for admission—but they will make your application more competitive. AP courses are college-level classes taught in high school, usually during junior and senior year, and culminate each May with subject exams. AP exams are typically a combination of multiple choice and free response questions and run two to three hours, and they're scored out of 5. Some language tests include an audio component.

That might sound like a lot of work for a score that isn't absolutely necessary—and only out of 5! But AP courses and exams can give both you and your college application a whole lot of power. AP classes on your high school transcript show admissions officers that you're academically engaged and willing to challenge yourself—that's what I mean when I talk about the rigor of your high school transcript. You can pursue subjects that you find compelling, and you will develop research and analytical skills that will help you succeed in college. AP exams will help you after you get into college, too. Many colleges give course credits for AP scores of 4 or 5. Walking onto campus with a few academic credits already in your pocket can potentially help you place out of prerequisite classes; it can free up your schedule to pursue an academic minor, an internship, or a part-time job. Several AP credits and careful academic planning can also help you graduate a semester or even a year early, which is one strategy for keeping the overall cost of your degree down.

As you chart your course through high school, find out what AP classes are available at your high school. There are 38 subject exams, but not every subject is taught at all high schools, and you'll need to know any courses you're required to take before entering an AP course (for example, you may need to take a couple of years of honors classes in Spanish to enroll in AP Spanish your senior year). While taking challenging courses is essential to building a college-ready high school transcript, overloading your schedule in one semester or year can cause a lot of stress and set up unnecessary obstacles to achieving the best grades possible. Choose AP subjects that interest you and in which you received good grades in introductory level courses. Balance your workload by taking one or two AP classes each semester in 11th and 12th grade, rather than trying to pursue an all-AP schedule all the time.

When you take an AP class, make a plan to prep for the exam by March 1.

When you take an AP class, make a plan to prep for the exam by March 1. The course will give you a deep dive into material covered on the test, but as with all standardized tests, you will benefit from getting familiar with the test format. You'll sit for the test in early May, so you'll need to schedule time to review class material and work practice questions within accurate time limits (along with all your other homework, extracurriculars, test prep, and down time!). Look at your AP exams as a chance to brag to admissions officers about your knowledge of subjects that excite you.

Top 5 Benefits of Taking AP Classes

1. **They will prep you for college.** AP classes can be as challenging as introductory college courses.
2. **They can help you rise to the top of the pile.** Prove to admissions officers that you're ready for college-level work.
3. **They make your transcript stronger.** Extra weight is given to AP grades at many high schools when determining your GPA.
4. **You can study what you love.** There are 38 AP subjects from a broad range of studies from Latin to Studio Art.
5. **You can get a head start on college requirements and save money.** High AP scores can earn you college credits without having to pay college tuition.

What's an International Baccalaureate (IB) Diploma? How do college admission counselors treat an IB diploma?

The International Baccalaureate Diploma Programme is another high school curriculum option that, like honors or AP classes, give you opportunities to challenge yourself academically and signal to admissions officers that you're capable of rigorous academic work. It is a specific curriculum and set of assessments completed in the final two years of high school, and is only available at some U.S. high schools that have been accredited by the International Baccalaureate. It was developed in Switzerland in the 1960s by an international coalition of educators, with the goal of creating a curriculum that prepares students for college-level academics that could be implemented globally. If you're a high school junior and this is the first time you're learning about the International Baccalaureate program, I don't want you to panic over a missed opportunity! Many U.S. high schools do not offer the IB program, but do offer other challenging classes and programs (like AP courses) that will give weight to your transcript. Going for an IB diploma is a decision you want to make with input from your parents and guidance counselor, possibly as early as 8th grade, as you will need to attend a high school that offers the program.

When students and parents ask about IB diplomas and college admissions, they're usually in one of two camps: either they're already pursuing an IB, often overseas, and are worried that American colleges and universities don't recognize its qualifications; or

> Most admissions professionals rank AP credits and IB credits on a college application equally.

they want to know if AP credits or IB credits are more impressive to admissions officers. I've got good news for everyone: admissions officers at U.S. schools are familiar with the International Baccalaureate and the high level of academic study and performance it entails, and most of the admissions professionals I've met in my time rank AP credits and IB credits on a college application equally. They both reflect a student who pursues academic achievement through the opportunities available—AP classes are more widely available to high school students in the United States than IB classes. The IB diploma may not be an option at your school, or it might not be the best curriculum for your learning style, but that won't count against you if your transcript includes honors and/or AP courses, or even specialized summer programs.

> **Some schools award college credits for IB subjects.**

If an IB diploma is an option for you, it's a unique opportunity that you should discuss with your high school guidance counselor, or a teacher you trust to honestly evaluate your academic potential. Individual colleges and universities have different policies regarding IB credits, but as with APs, some schools award college credits for IB subjects. There are also IB-specific scholarships available at universities worldwide, including almost sixty schools in the United States.

High School Testing Timeline

Extracurricular activities, school commitments, and other factors play into when and how you're going to prepare for the SAT and ACT. Folks, there's no perfect plan. But here's what I recommend for students going into their junior year.

- ☐ **Summer before junior year:** Prep for the SAT and take it in August or October for the first time.

- ☐ **October:** Take the PSAT.

- ☐ **November/December:** Take the SAT one more time.

- ☐ **February:** Start prepping for the ACT and take it for the first time.

- ☐ **April:** Take the ACT one more time.

- ☐ **May:** Study, and take your AP tests.

- ☐ **June:** Sign up for one to three SAT Subject Tests.

- ☐ **Summer before senior year:** You can take the SAT or ACT one more time if necessary. If you take a summer test, you'll receive scores in time for Early Action or Early Decision deadlines.

Chapter 3

High School Transcripts

CHAPTER 3
High School Transcripts

Colleges care about the classes you take every year until high school graduation. So should you sign up for AP Calculus and AP Physics the same year? Take it easy early on, and then pile on the challenging work junior year?

The general rule is to take five solid academic subjects a year in English, math, social studies, science and foreign language. My tips will help you choose the right high school classes each year, and understand how your GPA factors into college applications.

What should I be doing in 9th and 10th grades to prepare for the college admission process?

I love it when folks are ready to start thinking about the college admission process early! Planning ahead won't just set you up to succeed, it can also help make the process a lot less stressful. If you're reading this book in 9th or 10th grade, you are already ahead of the game.

First and foremost: Aim for academic awesomeness for all four years of high school. Great grades in college prep courses are a key part of your college application and scholarship dollars for school. Simply put, that means you should put in the time and effort your school work requires. Create study habits that work with your learning style and schedule. Tackle assignments that seem particularly challenging head on. That might mean that on a typical Tuesday night, you do the homework for your least favorite subject first and save your favorite subject for last. Or it might mean starting a project like an essay on Shakespeare or a science experiment early, so that you have time to ask for any help you might need and revise your work. Use these early years to identify the academic areas in which you need extra time and support, and you can set yourself up for success down the road. I know that high school is not always simple, though, and I share some advice on what you can do if you find that your best efforts are not adding up to a 4.0 grade point average later in this chapter.

When it comes to choosing classes, think of your freshman year as the foundation of your high school experience. Set long term goals for high school and break down the tasks and decisions that you will need to complete to achieve those goals. For example, consider the course subjects you enjoy and in which you excel. Are there opportunities to take advanced-level classes in those subjects in your junior and senior years? If so, find out what prerequisite courses or grades you need to earn a seat in those classes.

Your first two years of high school is also a good time to try out electives and extracurricular activities. Challenging yourself academically and earning good grades are important and will show any admission committee that you are achievement-driven and willing to work hard; pursuing interests outside of your required courses will show them that you are intellectually curious and eager to engage with your community. This is vital information for admission at competitive schools, where officers look for the energy and unique traits you will bring to campus, as well as academic excellence! I dig into electives later in this chapter, but I urge you to choose subjects that excite you, not what you think will impress an admission officer. Enthusiastic authenticity is impressive!

During your sophomore year, you may want to start some initial college research. If you have older siblings who are visiting college campuses, tag along! Browse online message boards, university websites and social media accounts, and pick up an annual guide like my *Best Colleges* book. Begin to imagine yourself on a college campus; what facilities and qualities will make you feel at home? Preliminary research can help you be efficient when you refine your list of target schools later on.

Finally, a note about standardized tests. You may want to consider taking SAT Subject Tests as early as the end of 9th grade, depending on the subjects you are taking (for example, if you are required to take biology during your freshman year, take the SAT Subject Test in biology in June of that year). You will have other opportunities to take these tests in 10th and 11th grade, and you won't know which subjects (if any) you will need for your college application until you know where you plan to apply. But knocking out a few SAT Subject Tests now (timed to when your class in that discipline is still fresh in your noggin) can give you more flexibility and decrease stress later on!

You *don't* need to start prepping for the SAT or ACT in 9th grade. Of course if you like practice, it won't hurt, but if you experience test anxiety it may be a distraction from focusing on your grades. If you do want to get a jump on your prep for these tests, I recommend taking a couple of practice exams during sophomore year, to get a sense of the differences between the ACT and SAT (see Chapter 2). If earning National Merit Scholar status is important to you, plan to prep for the PSAT during the summer between sophomore and junior year. You will take the PSAT in October of your junior year.

You *don't* need to start prepping for the SAT or ACT in 9th grade.

College-Bound:
Freshman & Sophomore Year Checklist

Freshman Year

☐ Focus on your grades so you can earn placement for more rigorous courses.

☐ Practice your study skills, identify support resources available, and ask for help if you need it.

☐ Get to know your school and community! Explore clubs, sports, volunteer opportunities, and more.

☐ Take any appropriate SAT Subject Tests.

Sophomore Year

☐ Continue to challenge yourself academically.

☐ Develop constructive relationships with your teachers.

☐ Get to know your school counselor.

☐ Commit to the activities that you really enjoy, and try to take on more responsibility.

☐ Take any appropriate SAT Subject Tests.

Summer Before Junior Year

☐ This is the perfect time to prep for the SAT and ACT.

☐ Begin your college research.

What should I be doing in 11th and 12th grades to prepare for the college admission process?

Hopefully, you're not surprised to hear that these years are absolutely crucial for your college application! Junior and senior year of high school, you want to take tough courses, get great grades, prep for your standardized tests, choose schools to which you want to apply, and demonstrate leadership in your extracurricular activities. So your first job is to manage your time well.

Put key dates in your calendar at the beginning of the school year to help stay on track:

Junior year
Standardized test dates—confirm your local dates for each test:
- PSAT (October)
- AP exams (May)
- SAT Subject tests (June)
- SAT (varies)
- ACT (varies)
- Midterms, finals, and any other major exam or project deadline dates that your teachers give you at the start of each term
- Local college fairs or dates when representatives from colleges that you are considering are visiting your high school (spring)
- Long weekends when you might want to plan to visit colleges (spring)

Senior year
Standardized test dates:
- Fall of senior year is your last chance to take or re-take the SAT or ACT.
- Make sure you leave enough time to get your scores back before submitting your applications!
- AP exams (May). While you will most likely have committed to a college by the time these exams roll around, some universities will give college credit for a score of 4 or 5, which can help you fill language requirements, skip prerequisites for more advanced courses, and even save a little money if tuition is charged by credit rather than by semester.
- Deadlines for the colleges and universities where you'll be submitting applications—especially if you're applying early!

- Financial aid deadlines. The Free Application for Federal Student Aid, or FAFSA, is available on October 1st each year, and I always recommend getting that in as early as possible.
- Midterms, finals, and any other major exam or project deadline dates that your teachers give you at the start of each term; your fall grades will be super important to the admission committee.
- College interviews

You'll have plenty of other deadlines and appointments to keep as you get into each year—setting up the major guideposts early will save you a lot of angst.

Your grades should be your first priority throughout junior year. Even if you faced some struggles or missteps in your first two years of high school, buckling down junior year can make a big difference. An upward trend in your grades will show admission officers that you've matured and can overcome challenges. If hard work and dedication aren't earning you the grades you want, ask your teacher if he or she can meet with you outside of class to review difficult material, form a study group, or find a tutor (your school may offer a free peer-tutoring program, or look online for affordable options). Your teachers and high school counselors want you to succeed, so don't be afraid to ask for help if you need it.

You'll most likely be taking the PSAT in October of your junior year. Your score report won't be shared with any colleges, but it will give you a clear idea of how your scores compare to everyone else who took the same test and areas where you want to improve. The PSAT is also used to qualify for the National Merit Scholarship Program, which is a good reason to get some practice in before you officially take the test. National Merit Scholarship Finalist or Semi-finalist status is a great achievement to include on your application, and you may earn some scholarship dough in the process.

Junior spring is the perfect time to begin researching and visiting colleges—just don't lose your focus on your schoolwork while you plan for your future! Revisit Chapter 1 for my advice on college research and campus visits.

By the summer before senior year, you're ready for the nitty-gritty test prep plans I cover in Chapter 2. Senior fall is your last chance to nail the SAT or ACT, which makes the summer before an excellent time to take a prep course and seek out extra practice on the sections of the test that you find most difficult.

Grades remain important—most colleges request copies of your final high school transcript, even if you've already been accepted. If your GPA takes a nose dive during senior year, you could enter college on academic probation, or even find your acceptance rescinded. That said, senior spring is a great time to take a lighter course load and really enjoy your electives.

Keep your nose to the grindstone in the fall of your senior year—even if your GPA kicks butt and you can check standardized tests off your to-do list, you'll need time to complete your applications and proofread them thoroughly. I break down each part of the application in Chapter 6, but the best advice for applications can't be repeated enough! Start early, do a little bit at a time, and proofread, proofread, proofread!

How to Get Better Grades

One bad test, month, or quarter doesn't have to sink your GPA. You can still end up where you want to be—if you take action now!

1. **Think of class like an opportunity to study.** Take great notes, pay attention, and ask questions. That in-class study time sure adds up!

2. **Start studying before you need to.** For big assignments, start small. Stay motivated by completing a small piece of the project every few days.

3. **Get rid of homework distractions.** Even a 3-second interruption (like the time it takes to glance down at your buzzing phone) has the power to derail the task you're working on.

4. **Use your old tests and quizzes to help you study.** It's also a good idea to look over your notes every night to make sure that you've got it.

5. **Ask for help when you need it.** Students who are willing to ask for a little help impress teachers, counselors, and colleges alike. Chat with your teachers after class, learn about any academic resources your school offers, or try a tutor.

6. **If you can teach it, you know it.** Get to the point that you're comfortable enough with the material that you can teach it to someone else.

College-Bound: Junior & Senior Year Checklist

Junior Year

☐ Take the SAT and ACT when you're ready.

☐ Balance schoolwork and outside-school interests.

☐ Take the most challenging courses available to you.

☐ Take the PSAT/NMSQT in October to qualify for a National Merit Scholarship and other scholarship opportunities.

☐ Start gathering teacher recommendations.

☐ Narrow your college list and try to visit one or two campuses while class is in session.

☐ Make a plan to prepare for AP exams in May and SAT Subject Tests in June.

☐ Learn about financial aid and available scholarships.

Summer Before Senior Year

☐ Start working on your application and prewriting college essays—they take longer than you think!

☐ Make a calendar of all your application deadlines so you can stay on track.

☐ If possible, consider visiting colleges that are on the top of your target list.

☐ If you are applying for Early Decision, you should take the SAT or ACT no later than September.

Senior Fall

- ☐ Apply early if you're a strong candidate.

- ☐ Wrap up your applications and stay on top of deadlines for apps, scholarships, and financial aid.

- ☐ Don't get senioritis! Senior grades matter—your first term grades will definitely be used in the admissions process.

- ☐ Complete your last SAT/ACT by December at the latest.

Senior Spring

- ☐ If you still have AP exams to take, study!

- ☐ Send thank-you notes to your recommenders.

- ☐ Get ready to celebrate! Spring is all about acceptance letters rolling in.

- ☐ Talk to friends, family, and counselors before making your final choice.

- ☐ Once you decide, don't look back! Read through your college's course catalog, and look forward to the next four years.

Is it better to have a B in an honors/AP course or an A in a regular/easier course?

This question is a favorite among parents! I can understand why. Most likely, you know the average test scores and GPA of the most recent incoming class at your dream school (this is information schools publish each year, and report to many publishers of college rankings). But those averages don't offer much insight into the courses in which accepted students earned those grades.

I know that reducing college admission to a handful of statistics is appealing. It seems to remove the mystery from the process—but I've mentioned that most admission officers tell me that they read applications holistically. That means they don't just look at a student's stats, they look at a full secondary school transcript, including grade trends over time and the difficulty of a student's classes (alongside all of your other application materials, of course!). When The Princeton Review collected school information for our book *The Best 382 Colleges, 2018 Edition*, nearly 90 percent of those schools reported that both an applicant's GPA and the rigor of his or her high school transcript are very important factors in their admissions decisions.

My advice: Take the most challenging courses available to you, and work hard to earn solid grades. It will show admission committees that you are intellectually curious, up for a challenge, and willing to work hard.

All that said, I know that at the same time you're studying for those awesome grades, you're probably also preparing for standardized tests, participating in extracurricular activities, perhaps captaining a varsity team or working an after-school job, plus finding time to spend with your family and friends. It's important to avoid burning out—take it from me, stress is not a key ingredient for success! Make sure that you take some down time each week, and ask for the help you need from teachers, advisors, parents, and tutors. I want you to challenge yourself, not torture yourself!

My school doesn't publish class rank. Will that hurt my application?

I've got good news for you here! Lots of high schools are ditching class rank, and in response, many colleges and universities are making adjustments to the way they view admission factors. More than half of the students in the class of 2018 at both Swarthmore College and Dartmouth College were admitted without their class rank represented in their applications.[1]

While class rank may help provide useful context for your high school transcript to admission officers, it doesn't really fit in with the holistic application review process that most counselors describe. You're not just a number, you're an individual with a unique set of personality traits and experiences to contribute to a campus community. The folks in the admission know that, and many of them will look at your application that way.

> You're not just a number, you're an individual with a unique set of personality traits and experiences to contribute to a campus community. The folks in the admission know that, and many of them will look at your application that way.

One important note about class rank: If you are applying to a school within a state university system, I strongly encourage you to double check the specific school's admission practices. Class rank remains an important factor in Texas, for example, where the top 10 percent of in-state high school students are automatically admitted to all schools in the state university system.[2] Typically, these systems have policies in place for evaluating applicants from high schools that do not publish class rank.

1   https://www.washingtonpost.com/news/grade-point/wp/2015/07/13/
    high-schools-are-doing-away-with-class-rank-what-does-that-mean-for-college-admissions
2   http://www.legis.state.tx.us/billlookup/History.aspx?LegSess=80R&Bill=HB78&Sort=A

What carries more weight on a college application: GPA or test scores?

Your GPA and the rigor of your high school courses are without a doubt the most important factors on your application—but test scores run a close third. Over 70 percent of the colleges and universities we surveyed for *The Best 382 Colleges 2018 Edition* reported that standardized test scores are "important" or "very important" in their evaluation of applicants.

What does that mean for you? Practice and prep! Taking a free practice SAT or ACT will help you figure out which test is best for you, and help you identify the areas in which you might want to put in a little extra effort to get the score you want. You can find the average standardized test scores of the most recently admitted class at your dream schools online, which will help you set your goal score.

Build time into your schedule to prepare for whichever test you choose, and find prep tools that fit your needs and schedule. There are many, many test prep options available to suit a wide range of learning styles, and student schedules, at a variety of prices. I'm a longtime test prep teacher for The Princeton Review. There are over 4,000 teachers and tutors here! Whether it's a book, online/classroom course or one-on-one tutoring, choose the option best for you. Your high school or public library may offer free or discounted resources, and your high school counselor can offer recommendations as well.

As I mentioned in Chapter 2, some schools are test optional, which means they will consider your test scores if you submit them, but your scores are not required for you to be considered for admission. If your first choice college is test optional, you may still want to consider preparing for and taking the SAT or ACT—these scores are often important when you're applying for scholarships.

Which electives should I take?

I've been telling you what you should and need and might want to do to craft a competitive college application for pages and pages now, but here I'm going to stop. Take whatever electives look interesting to you. Electives give you opportunities to explore new subjects and skills, and having a clear sense of your strengths and weaknesses will help you succeed in college and your career. If you're invested in the subject at hand, it will be less stressful to earn good grades in that subject. Your academic grades will receive closer scrutiny inside college admission offices than your elective grades, but obviously they will still factor into your overall GPA.

My one recommendation when choosing electives is that you stick with at least one or two subjects for more than one semester—chances are, electives are offered at introductory and more advanced levels at your high school. Sticking with a subject through ascending levels will show admissions officers that you're capable of making a professional commitment and that you actively pursue subjects that you are interested in.

That doesn't mean that you're committed to all the electives you choose in 9th grade for four years. Taking a variety of introductory electives will expose you to new interests and talents, whether you prefer studio art or software development or journalism. Then move on to intermediate and advanced courses in the elective subjects that you most enjoy. If you are facing a particularly challenging semester with a heavy academic course load and preparing for standardized tests on the horizon, you might consider a less intensive elective during that time. Time management is essential to maintain good grades.

How do admission counselors view applications from public school students vs. private school students?

All colleges accept and enroll students from both public and private schools every year.

School	% of first-year students enrolled in fall 2016 from public high schools
Boston University	64%
George Washington University	70%
New York University	59%
Ohio State University Columbus	85%
Stanford University	59%
Syracuse University	66%
University of Arizona	90%
University of California Los Angeles	75%
University of Colorado Boulder	88%
University of Pennsylvania	60%
University of Virginia	70%

Admissions officers understand that the range of resources on offer to students varies wildly from one high school to the next, whether you attend a public high school in suburban Texas, a charter school in downtown Chicago, a boarding school in Connecticut, or you're homeschooled in Oregon. Part of the work of college admissions, recruitment, and enrollment includes evaluating an application in the context of the student's academic environment. It's up to you, the applicant, to take advantage of the opportunities at hand, both for your own enrichment and to help you represent your best self on your college applications.

Private high schools do typically offer a rich variety of academics, electives, and extracurricular activities; and favorable student-teacher and student-counselor ratios. For students, that means many options for experiences and accomplishments that will make for strong college applications, and lots of institutional support for pursuing those opportunities and crafting those applications. If this sounds like your high school experience, count yourself lucky.

If you attend a public high school, you're in the vast majority of college applicants, and you have many different paths to college acceptance regardless of the resources immediately available in your school. Admissions officers are not looking for a laundry list of achievements any more than they're looking for a set of sterile statistics. They're looking at how all the elements of an application come together to show the maturity, self-reliance, and character of the student behind the application.

How do I address my high school disciplinary record on my application?

If you have any significant disciplinary or legal issues on your high school record—think suspension, not detention—you should acknowledge it in your college application. Transparency here will show that you are responsible and mature, and if you try to hide past infractions from admissions officers only to have them turn up on your high school transcript, you're only doing yourself a disservice.

> Avoid making excuses or sounding defensive, and focus on what has changed since that incident.

You will most likely have an opportunity to explain yourself in writing within your primary essay or any supporting questions on the school's application, or you may choose to speak to it in your college interview (or both). Avoid making excuses or sounding defensive, and focus on what has changed since that incident. How have you grown? What did you learn from the experience? (Spoiler: "I learned not to get caught" is not a strong message to go with here.) Don't think of any blemishes on your record as liabilities—look at them as opportunities to show your maturity and capacity for learning from mistakes.

Whether you plan to write or speak about any issues in your past, you will need a few practice rounds. You should get feedback from someone you trust on any college essay—I go into more depth on admission essays in Chapter 6—but I strongly recommend working with your guidance counselor on the best context for disciplinary issues on your application. Write a couple of drafts, and go over talking points with your counselor to get prepped for your admissions interview (even if interviews are optional for admission to your dream school, this is a case where making a personal connection can really help you). In exceptional cases, a college might contact your school for more details, so you want to be sure that you and your counselor are aligned on the circumstances and outcome of any disciplinary action. This advice also applies if you want to address inconsistent grades.

My school is different (e.g., my GPA is out of 9.0; AP/ honors are the same classes; I get written reports instead of letter grades). How will I compare to applicants from "regular" schools?

If you've already read my answers in this chapter to the questions about class rank and private vs. public school, you can probably guess what I have to say here: colleges recognize that not all high schools use the same evaluation process. High school administrators and faculty, too, recognize that the quirks of their curriculum may need to be translated to college admission offices. Particularly for different GPA scales or grading systems, your high school probably has an alternative GPA formula in place, or in the case of non-letter grades, a formal statement explaining how students demonstrate they meet academic benchmarks. Your high school guidance counselor, or a teacher with experience writing recommendations, should be in a position to explain to you how any questions or discrepancies have been addressed by past applicants.

While a typical evaluation rubrics and class labels like honors vs. AP vs. advanced are not a detriment to your application, they won't act as a cover for low grades or easy classes, either. No matter how your high school curriculum is structured, you need good grades in challenging classes to be a competitive college applicant.

Chapter 4

Extracurricular Activities

Extracurricular Activities

I know you want to impress colleges with your accomplishments in the classroom, but your academics aren't the full picture of who you really are. Yes, colleges want bright students. But even more, they want bright, well-rounded students. That's where your extracurricular activities come in.

Grades and test scores are very important, but so is what you choose to do on your own time. Admissions officers are looking to create a class made up of students with diverse interests and backgrounds. They'll look closely at your extracurriculars to get a sense of the person you are and what you care about.

How do college admission officers view extracurricular activities within an application?

The core of your college application is comprised of your GPA, your high school transcript, and your standardized test scores. Taken together, these two statistics and one list of courses convey your capacity for seeking out and conquering academic challenges. But they don't say very much about your personality or non-academic interests (though this may come through in your choice of electives, depending on what is available at your high school). That's what admissions officers look for in your list of extracurricular activities. You want that list to show that you are engaged with the world outside the classroom, and that you are able to articulate how you spend your time.

> Keep at least one activity, sport, or job from 10th grade through graduation.

Extracurricular activities on your college application include any school-affiliated, non-academic activity, like sports, clubs, or performances. You can also include any organized activities you do outside of school, like music lessons, community service, or participating in a youth group. Seasonal and part-time jobs count, too. Your list of activities may show that you're well-rounded and have a range of interests; admissions officers will also be looking for consistency and leadership. If you can keep at least one activity, sport, or job from 10th grade through graduation, you'll show that you are committed to the pursuits and people that are important to you. Taking a leadership position or otherwise demonstrating that your responsibilities progressively increased over the course of your job or involvement with an activity or community is one of the best things you can do to show maturity and accountability on your college application.

Which activities do colleges view most favorably?

I suspect that you'd have a hard time getting a single list of "ideal" college activities from any college admission officer—imagine how boring the world would be if everyone who attended college did exactly the same extracurricular activities! Plus, if you force yourself to pursue something you don't genuinely enjoy, you're less likely to stick with it, to take on additional responsibilities pertaining to it, or write a compelling college essay about it. So the first rule of choosing an extracurricular that a college will view favorably is that YOU have to view it favorably.

Of course, it's still very useful to consider your extracurricular options from an admission counselor's perspective. This will help you put your activities in context on your application and highlight the skills and experiences from each activity that will make your application stronger. For admissions officers, playing on your high school basketball team conveys more than your love for the game, writing for your school newspaper conveys more than your passion for the written word, and your regular babysitting gig conveys more than your interest in earning spending money. Playing a sport shows that you understand teamwork, strategic thinking, and healthy competition. Pursuing a creative, intellectual, or technical project shows that you're self-aware, curious, and motivated. Maintaining a part-time job demonstrates responsibility, a sense of professionalism, and entrepreneurial motivation. Any combination of these qualities makes for a competitive college applicant—and a contributing campus citizen.

> For admissions officers, playing on your high school basketball team conveys more than your love for the game.

Find and commit to the extracurricular activities that you find meaningful, and look at your extracurricular list like an admissions officer once you're crafting your application. Maybe your primary extracurricular activity began with school requirements, like sports or community service, and led to more significant, long-term participation. Describing how you went from obligated to excited about a particular activity is a great story for a short application essay (when required) or an admissions interview. If the sport or activity that inspires you isn't offered at your school, you can seek out external resources, like community center classes or club sports. This provides you with examples of your independence, ambition, and time management skills.

Setting yourself up for a strong college application does take some planning, but it's best to begin with what matters to you, not to a theoretical future admissions panel. By staying engaged with academics and extracurriculars, you're providing yourself with opportunities for personal growth and self-awareness—qualities that appeal to colleges.

10 Smart Summer Activities

1. **Participate in a specialized high school program.** Explore future careers, develop leadership skills, and get a taste of college life.
2. **Take a college class.** Many colleges offer summer programs where high school students come to campus to take classes and live in the dorms.
3. **Find a summer program at a local school or community college.** Save money by living at home and attending college classes as a commuter student.
4. **Get a job.** Your work history demonstrates your initiative and responsibility, which impress colleges.
5. **Create your own project.** Turn your interests and talents into a summer-long project such as practicing creative writing and submitting your work to journals that publish the work of high school students.
6. **Become an entrepreneur.** Start a business with friends that offers a service to your community.
7. **Volunteer locally.** Commit to volunteering for a few hours a week from now through your senior year.
8. **Find a job-shadowing opportunity.** Soak up the atmosphere by observing and doing small tasks in a professional setting to get an idea of what a specific field is like.
9. **Start your test prep.** Keep your brain in tip-top shape by picking up a prep book, taking an online course, or finding a tutor to help you manage your time.
10. **Make college visits.** Take a college road trip with friends and family or do it virtually from the comfort of your own couch on YouTube.

Does having a job carry as much weight as school-related extracurricular activities?

Absolutely! On a college application, an after-school job conveys that you rise to responsibilities and challenges. Your classes and grades should always come first, and if you're considering applying for a job in high school, you should feel comfortable with the amount of time and flexibility you have for your homework. If an employer is willing to ask a high school student to sacrifice school or study time for work, they probably shouldn't hire high school students. If you're already managing a challenging school/work schedule, you've taken on a great deal of responsibility, and I'd encourage you to address any time management issues with your high school guidance counselor.

Working part-time while in high school might sometimes feel like you're missing out on both extracurricular opportunities and fun, but it's incredibly valuable for your future—in college and beyond. It might not always feel like much when you're stacking boxes or serving coffee, but each work experience leads to the next, so congratulations on entering the working world a little ahead of your peers. No matter what you do for work, there's a way to frame it strategically on your college application. For your essays and interviews, cherry-pick examples from your work experience to demonstrate that you are accountable to yourself and others, capable of constructive collaboration, and have developed your communication skills. Highlight moments of accomplishment and take pride in your work (even if you'd rather be playing video games during most of your shift).

If you hold a job in high school due to financial necessity, don't be afraid to make that clear on your application. Your experience can help you demonstrate how you handle obstacles, course-correct when work or schedules don't go as planned, and accept responsibility. Admissions officers know as well as you do that tuition is expensive, so working to earn money for tuition shows them how motivated you are to pursue higher education.

What about "grit"?

"Grit" is a buzzword that has been popular among educators and admissions officers in recent years. My own opinion is that "grit," an amorphous quality comprised of character and commitment, is great, but it's not actually a new element for college applications—admissions officers have been looking for it in candidates for a long time. It is commendable that education institutions are making attempts to quantify, measure, and develop "grit" in students, but I think it comes through on college applications whether we have a specific definition and measurement or not.

> All of the advice in this book is intended to help you see your application, and yourself, as a whole, not a collection of statistics and checkboxes.

It's my belief that a college application adds up to more than the sum of its parts—ultimately, your grades, test scores, recommendations, extracurricular activities, essays, interviews, and supplemental material tell a story about you. All of the advice in this book is intended to help you see your application, and yourself, as a whole, not a collection of statistics and checkboxes. When you are able to put your achievements and your passions together effectively, the story your college application tells is about your character, your interest in challenging yourself, and your ability to persevere.

By taking the most challenging classes available to you, taking advantage of resources and help to earn the highest grades and test scores possible; by building positive relationships with your recommenders; by articulating your interests, experiences, and growth through essays—you're showing college admission officers that you've got "grit."

Admissions Advantage or Life Advantage?

Just about everything you do to prepare for college has bigger life implications, too.

1. When you work hard in your classes in high school, you become better educated.

2. When you find and commit yourself to activities you enjoy, you discover your talents, learn to work with other people, and enjoy life outside of the classroom.

3. When you learn how to do something for yourself without relying on your parents, you become more independent and better prepared to live on your own.

4. When you find a subject that interests you and dive in to learn more, you see for yourself just how rewarding learning can be when you let your interests take you there.

5. When you struggle in a class and approach your teacher for help, you learn how to advocate for yourself and how to seek out assistance when you need it.

6. When you try your best and still come up short, you learn how to handle that failure or disappointment, learn from it, and then move on.

7. When you take all of these lessons with you to college, you get more out of the overall experience.

Chapter 5

Financial Aid & Scholarships

CHAPTER 5
Financial Aid & Scholarships

For more than 25 years, average college costs have annually risen higher than the rate of inflation. Now more than 60 colleges have a sticker price (tuition, fees, room and board) that's over $60,000 a year. Those numbers sound scary, and I often hear families make assumptions like, "We can't afford private schools," or "We'll never qualify for aid." Be careful—aid assumptions like those tend to work against you when it comes to paying for college.

Assuming your family can't pay for some (or any) colleges just takes options off the table. You may not be as motivated to work hard to get in. You may also eliminate certain colleges that are right for you, which are often the schools most likely to give you aid! The bottom line is that you won't know what your financial obligation will be until after you are accepted, apply for financial aid, and receive your financial aid award letter. So, as you factor the cost for college into your search, make no assumptions. Plan well, choose the right colleges, and apply for any aid that's available to you. In this chapter I show you how.

What is the FAFSA?

You'll hear about the FAFSA a whole lot during the college admissions process. This is the Free Application for Federal Student Aid. It's a long form that collects student and parent financial information and is used to determine the student's eligibility for financial aid. Even if you don't think you're eligible, you should still submit the form, just in case—you have nothing to lose.

When applying for college, you do not need to complete the FAFSA for each school where you plan to apply. You will be able to list up to ten schools on the application to receive the relevant information. You will need to complete the FAFSA each year you require aid. The form is updated each year and made available on October 1, for use in the following academic year. The FAFSA is available online, on paper, or as a downloadable PDF at fafsa.ed.gov. College financial aid deadlines vary. I strongly recommend submitting your FAFSA at the same time as your application for admission, and submitting it as soon as possible after October 1 each year thereafter.

> Crafting an appeal is a delicate art, and should only be undertaken if you have a strong case for revisiting your aid decision.

The financial information you enter on the FAFSA will cover the amount of money you and your parents or guardians made during the calendar year two years before you enter college—this is called the base income year on the FAFSA. For a student entering college directly after high school, financial aid eligibility will be based on their family's financial situation during 10th grade second semester and 11th grade first semester. Sometimes, careful planning can increase your eligibility for aid: for example, if either parent receives a bonus at the end of the base income year, they might consider deferring it to January of the following year, to avoid increasing their base income on the FAFSA. If your family has experienced a decrease in income between the base income year and your FAFSA submission, you may be able to address the change directly with the college of your choice by appealing the school's financial aid decision. Crafting an appeal is a delicate art, and should only be undertaken if you have a strong case for revisiting your aid decision.

Average Cost of College

Average cost of a year's tuition, room and board, and fees in 2017- 2018

Private College: $46,950

Public (In-State) College: $20,770

*College Board, *Trends in College Pricing, 2017*

When you complete the FAFSA, you will receive a Student Aid Report that summarizes the financial information you provided and shows your Expected Family Contribution (EFC), or the amount your family will be responsible for paying toward your college costs. (I go into EFC in more detail on the next page). Your Student Aid Report also will show your eligibility for different types of federal student aid. You may also be eligible for state financial aid and/or for aid granted directly by the school. And, if you're not eligible for federal financial aid, you may still be eligible for state aid. Federal aid is based on adjusted gross income and assets (like property and investments). Some states base financial aid eligibility on taxable income and do not take other assets into account. All fifty states have need-based aid programs and about half offer merit-based aid, which is awarded based on your academic record and test scores instead of on your financial situation, as well. In most cases, to be eligible for state aid, you must attend a private or public college or university within your state of residence. In some states, aid is awarded on a first-come, first-served basis, so it benefits you to apply early.

I know it sounds complicated, but financial aid is just another part of the college admission process that we can crack through research and planning.

What is my Expected Family Contribution?

> I always discourage families from crossing schools off their list based on sticker price early in the application process.

When you complete the FAFSA, the federal financial aid methodology determines how much your family can afford to put toward your college education based on their income and assets. This is the Expected Family Contribution amount on your Student Aid Report. Your EFC is the same no matter where you go to school, or how much that school costs. The total cost of any college includes tuition and fees, room and board, personal expenses, books and supplies, and travel—as determined by each college or university. The difference between the total cost of attendance and your EFC is called your "need." Colleges and universities offer a wide range of aid packages to cover that need, which is why I always discourage families from crossing schools off their list based on sticker price early in the application process.

You can find financial aid and EFC "calculators" online, in which you can enter a sampling of the information you will provide on your FAFSA and find estimated college costs based on your financial situation. These can be helpful in getting oriented in college planning, but take the resulting figures with a healthy pinch of salt. Calculator methodology varies from site to site and the results are not guaranteed, even when the calculator is hosted on the college's own website.

What's the CSS/Financial Aid PROFILE?

CSS stands for College Scholarship Service. This is another form that collects your financial information to determine your financial need for college, and it goes into more detail than the FAFSA does. Your state and/or some private colleges may require the CSS PROFILE in addition to the FAFSA, while public institutions typically rely exclusively on the FAFSA to make financial aid decisions. The CSS PROFILE is created by the College Board (the same entity that writes the SAT, SAT Subject Tests, and AP Exams), and unlike the FAFSA, it entails application fees. Colleges that require the CSS PROFILE are not trying to punish you with extra forms and fees. These schools have additional financial aid resources beyond federal funds, and their financial aid officers want to have a detailed picture of your finances so they can try to help you cover your college costs. Institutions that rely on the FAFSA use the federal methodology to determine your eligibility for aid, while those that use the CSS most likely have their own institutional methodology. You can contact a specific school's Financial Aid Office with any questions about their methodology and decision-making process.

When you complete the CSS PROFILE (which you can do on collegeboard. org), instead of a Student Aid Report, you will receive a Data Confirmation Report summarizing your information and confirming which schools received it.

Survey Says

85% estimate their college costs will be more than $50,000

*Results of The Princeton Review's 2017 College Hopes & Worries Survey of college applicants and parents of college applicants.

What financial information do I need to apply for financial aid using the FAFSA and/or the CSS PROFILE?

For the FAFSA, you will need:

1. Completed federal tax return for the base income year (two calendar years before you or your student will enter college)

2. W-2 forms for the base income year

3. Records of any untaxed income for the base income year, if applicable. Examples include social security, welfare, tax-exempt interest

4. Bank statements for the base income year

5. Brokerage statements for the base income year, if applicable

6. Mortgage statements for any properties other than your primary residence for the base income year, if applicable

7. Student's social security number (and driver's license number if the student has one)

8. Any financial statements or corporate tax returns for businesses owned by parents or entrepreneurial applicants for the base income year

9. Other investment statements and records for the base income year

10. Records of child support paid or received during the base income year

For the CSS PROFILE, in addition to the 10 items above, you will also need:

11. Records of medical and dental expenses paid during the base income year

12. Records of any post-secondary tuition paid or that will be paid during the academic year before the year for which you are applying for aid

13. Records of any educational loan payments made or to be made during the two calendar years prior to the year for which you are applying for aid

14. Mortgage statements for your primary residence for the base income year, if applicable

15. Financial aid awarded to any member of your household, if applicable, for the academic year prior to the year for which you are applying for aid

How does the financial aid application process differ from the admission process?

	Admissions	Financial Aid
Application	The Common Application OR The Coalition Application OR School's own application	FAFSA CSS/PROFILE if required State form if required School's own form if required
Decisions based on	Test scores if required GPA Rigor of high school courses Recommendations Essays Extracurriculars Supplemental application material	Yours and your guardians' financial picture
Deadlines *confirm exact deadlines for both application and financial aid with the schools on your list*	Regular decision: Typically Jan. 1 Early decision: Typically Nov. 15	The latest date you can file a FAFSA is June 30th of the academic year for which you are applying, but most colleges request that all aid forms are completed with your admission application. I recommend submitting your financial aid forms ASAP after October 1.

I recommend submitting your financial aid forms ASAP after October 1.

What is in my financial aid package?

Your financial aid award letter will include details on the combination of aid that the school can offer to meet your demonstrated financial need. There are three types of aid:

Grants and Scholarships

Money that you won't have to pay back! Grants may be funded by the federal government, the state, or the college. Grants are tax-free. Most scholarships are awarded by the college or university, and may include eligibility criteria, like meeting a GPA threshold or participating in an extracurricular leadership development program. Some schools are more transparent than others about the amount of grant money available to students, which is usually based on the school's endowment and aid policy. Some schools guarantee grants or scholarships for accepted students who meet GPA and test score thresholds. Some find creative ways to give aid to all of their students. Cooper Union in New York, NY, awards every student who attends a scholarship to cover half of their tuition, and all students are automatically considered for additional merit aid. Berea College in Berea, KY, awards every admitted student a Tuition Promise Scholarship, which is combined with financial aid to cover the full cost of tuition. (Keep in mind that tuition does not include room and board, personal expenses, or travel.) At Guilford College in Greensboro, NC, every student in the class of 2017 received some amount of scholarship money. These are just three examples of schools with strong public track records of awarding generous financial aid.

Student Loans

Education loans are typically taken out by the student rather than their parents. Federal and state loans are often subsidized, and below-market interest rates guaranteed, by the government. You won't have to pay back the loans until you graduate, and many loan programs offer income-based repayment options. Even with favorable borrowing and repayment terms, be wary of accruing debt in college, and take out private unsubsidized loans as little as possible.

> Even with favorable borrowing and repayment terms, be wary of accruing debt in college, and take out private unsubsidized loans as little as possible.

Federal Work-Study

> The money you earn through a work-study job goes to tuition and/or living expenses.

This is a program through which the government provides money to the school to fund part-time jobs on campus for students. The money you earn through a work-study job goes to tuition and/or living expenses. It's also an opportunity to gain valuable work experience—many schools guarantee jobs to students who are eligible for work-study, and these experiences can help you find more lucrative summer employment and/or build your resume. The financial aid office will have a list of open positions and guidance on applying; jobs will likely run the gamut from food prep in the cafeteria to handling confidential information in the development office.

8 Quick Tips for Getting Financial Aid

1. **Learn how financial aid works.** The more and the sooner you know about how need-based aid eligibility is determined, the better you can take steps to maximize such eligibility.

2. **Apply for financial aid no matter what your circumstances.** Some merit-based aid can only be awarded if the applicant has submitted financial aid application forms.

3. **Don't wait until the student is accepted to apply for financial aid.** Do it when applying for admission.

4. **Complete all the required aid applications.** All students seeking aid must submit the FAFSA (Free Application for Federal Student Aid); other forms may also be required. Check with each college to see what's required and when.

5. **Get the best scores you can on the SAT or ACT.** They are used not only in decisions for admission but can also impact financial aid. If your scores and other stats exceed the school's admission criteria, you are likely to get a better aid package than a marginal applicant.

6. **Apply strategically to colleges.** Your chances of getting aid will be better at schools that have generous financial aid budgets. (Check the Financial Aid Ratings for various schools on PrincetonReview.com.)

7. **Don't rule out any school as too expensive.** A generous aid award from a pricey private school can make it less costly than a public school with a lower sticker price.

8. **Take advantage of education tax benefits.** A dollar saved on taxes is worth the same as a dollar in scholarship aid. Look into Coverdells, 529 Plans, education tax credits, and loan deductions.

*From *Paying for College Without Going Broke*, 2018 Edition by Kalman Chany

What is the difference between need-based and merit-based financial aid?

"Need-based" financial aid is determined by your household finances, and is intended to cover the difference between your Expected Family Contribution and the total cost of attending college.

When you are researching application deadlines for your prospective colleges, make a note of any scholarships for which you might be a competitive candidate and their deadlines.

"Merit-based" financial aid is determined by the college or university that has accepted you based on your academic, athletic, or artistic talent, and may be awarded regardless of your demonstrated need (that means it can lower your Expected Family Contribution). Merit-based aid is typically referred to as a grant or a scholarship, or either, depending on the awarding institution. When you are researching deadlines for each of the schools where you plan to apply, make a note of any scholarships for which you might be a competitive candidate and their deadlines, as in some instances specific scholarships may have earlier application deadlines than regular admission or financial aid applications.

How do I look for scholarships?

The best place to look for scholarships is within the institutions to which you are applying. Most schools work to fund and award scholarships and grants based on a variety of criteria, and many automatically consider you for merit-based grants or scholarships when you apply for admission and submit your FAFSA. If you want to pursue a scholarship, though, don't assume it will be a snap: ask the admissions officers at the school of your choice how many scholarships are awarded each year; how many students apply for scholarships (or the one scholarship you have your eye on); and if the scholarship is renewable. Some scholarships are only for first-year students. Some renew each year, but only if you maintain a certain GPA, pursue a specific major, or continue to compete on the varsity basketball team (for example).

A few good places to look for scholarships outside of colleges and universities are your city/town/municipal government, your parents' or guardians' employers, and any professional or philanthropic organizations to which they might belong. Scholarships from sources outside the college or university account for less than 5 percent of the financial aid awarded in the United States. That is still a lot of money

> Scholarships from sources outside the college or university account for less than 5 percent of the financial aid awarded in the United States.

(a total of $181 billion in student aid was available in 2017), but overall your odds of using an outside scholarship to pay for college are low.

If you are considering using a scholarship search service that charges a fee, please please please vet it very carefully. While some of these services are legit and have been a boon for their users, some are simply charging for information you can find for free with a little legwork.

How do I save/pay for college?

To be completely frank, this topic deserves a book of its own, and happily, my friend Kal Chany has written that book, *Paying for College Without Going Broke*. It's packed with investment tips for saving money for college and line-by-line strategies for completing the FAFSA to help you maximize your eligibility for financial aid. In lieu of trying to pass myself off as a financial advisor here, I'm presenting an overview of calculating college costs in the future and some helpful tips that will get you oriented around college expenses.

If you're reading this book in high school, hopefully your family has already started saving when it comes to your college tuition. Don't worry if that's not your situation; there are a lot of options for paying for college, especially if you focus on earning high test scores and grades. While financial aid is based primarily on demonstrated need, applicants who are especially desirable to a college because of their strong academic performance or athletic or artistic talent may receive preferential packaging—basically, a more lucrative financial aid package, whether it's a higher total amount or is comprised of more grants or scholarships than loans.

No matter when you plan to attend college, if you're not already saving, start now. Every little bit helps, and if you can put your money into a high-yield investment or savings account, it will earn compound interest—that means more money for college. If your parents are saving for you, their accounts and investments should be in their names—putting that money in your name could impact your eligibility for financial aid.

Calculate Your Costs

According to the College Board, as of 2017, the average sticker price (tuition, fees, room and board) for one year at a public four-year college was $20,770. One year at a private four-year college will cost more than twice that, at $46,950. The current rate at which college costs are increasing is about 4 percent per year—believe it or not, this has fallen off from trends indicating a 6 percent annual increase in recent years. While we can't predict the future with perfect accuracy, we can use these figures to calculate useful estimates.

Year	Avg Annual Cost: Public	Avg Annual Cost: Private
2018	$21,600	$48,828
2019	$22,464	$50,781.12
2020	$23,362.56	$52,812.36
2021	$24,297.06	$54,924.85
2022	$25,268.94	$57,121.84

It's worth noting that we're looking at average figures, and many private colleges already have annual sticker prices higher than $57,000. The more you can save for college, the more options will be available to you. You do not need to be a millionaire to obtain a college degree, however—during the 2016-2017 academic year, 79 percent of college students received some form of financial aid.

20 Financial Aid Terms You Need To Know

1. **Financial Aid:** A general term used to refer to a variety of programs funded by the federal and state governments as well as the individual schools to assist students with their educational costs. While the names may vary, financial aid comes in three basic forms: (1) gift aid (grants and scholarships) that does not have to be paid back (2) student loans, and (3) work-study jobs.

2. **Cost of Attendance:** A figure, estimated by the school, that includes the cost of tuition, fees, room, board, books, and supplies as well as an allowance for transportation and personal expenses. This figure is compared to the Expected Family Contribution to determine a student's aid eligibility.

3. **Expected Family Contribution (EFC):** The amount of money the family is expected to contribute for the year toward the student's cost of attendance. This figure is compared to the Cost of Attendance to determine a student's aid eligibility.

4. **Parent's Contribution:** The amount of money the parent(s) are expected to contribute for the year toward the student's Cost of Attendance.

5. **Student's Contribution:** The amount of money the student is expected to contribute for the year toward his or her cost of attendance.

6. **Need:** The amount of aid a student is eligible to receive. This figure is calculated by subtracting the Expected Family Contribution from the Cost of Attendance.

7. **Need Analysis Forms:** Aid applications used to calculate the expected family contribution. The most common need analysis forms are: the Free Application for Federal Student Aid (FAFSA) and the CSS/Financial Aid PROFILE form. Consult the individual school's financial aid filing requirements to determine which form(s) are required for that particular school.

8. **Free Application for Federal Student Aid (FAFSA):** The need analysis document written by the U.S. Department of Education. This form is required for virtually all students seeking financial aid including the unsubsidized Stafford loan.

9. **Student Aid Report (SAR):** The multi-page report that is issued to students who have filed a completed FAFSA.

10. **CSS/Financial Aid PROFILE:** A need analysis application created and processed by the College Board. Also known as the CSS PROFILE or the PROFILE form.

11. **Institutional Forms:** Supplemental forms required by the individual schools to determine aid eligibility.

12. **Gift Aid:** Financial aid, usually a grant or scholarship, that does not have to be paid back and that does not involve employment.

13. **Grants:** Gift aid that is generally based on need. The programs can be funded by the federal and state governments as well as the individual schools.

14. **Pell Grant:** A federally funded need-based grant program for first-time undergraduate students (i.e., the student has not as yet earned a bachelor's or first professional degree). Funds from this program are generally awarded to lower- and lower-middle-income families. Years ago, this program was called the Basic Educational Opportunity Grant (BEOG).

15. **Scholarships:** Gift aid that is usually based on merit or a combination of need and merit.

16. **Self-Help:** The portion of the aid package relating to student loans and/or work-study.

17. **Direct Loan Program:** Formerly known as the Stafford Student Loan program, this federally funded program provides low-interest loans to undergraduate and graduate students. In most cases, repayment does not begin until six months after the student graduates or leaves school and there are no interest charges while the student is in school. For new loans disbursed after June 30, 2006, the interest rate is fixed. (Prior loans had variable rates.) There are two types of Direct loans: subsidized and unsubsidized. The subsidized Direct loan is need-based and the government pays the interest while the student is in school. The unsubsidized Direct loan is non-need-based and can be taken out by virtually all students. In many cases, students can elect to let the interest accumulate until after they graduate.

18. **Parents Loans for Undergraduate Students (PLUS):** A federally sponsored educational loan program in which parents can borrow up to the total cost of attendance minus any financial aid received for each child in an undergraduate program. Eligibility is not based on need.

19. **Perkins Loan Program:** This federally funded need-based program provides low interest loans to undergraduate and graduate students and is administered by the school's financial aid office. In most cases, repayment does not begin until nine months after the student graduates or leaves school and there are no interest charges while the student is in school. The fixed interest rate is currently 5 percent.

20. **Federal Work Study (FWS):** A federally funded aid program that provides jobs for students. Eligibility is based on need.

What is a need-blind school?

"Need-blind" means a college or university makes admission decisions without taking into account an applicant's financial situation. A school may also be "need-sensitive" or "need-aware," which means that finances are considered in admissions in order to ensure that the school will be able to offer financial aid to those students who need it. While taking finances out of the admissions process may sound like a fairer process given how hard you're working on your grades and test scores, it can be disappointing for students who are accepted but find their demonstrated financial need is not met by their financial aid package.

For applicants, a need-blind admission policy is most meaningful when it is combined with a commitment from the school to meet every accepted students' demonstrated need. In most cases, these policies only apply to U.S. applicants, due to the college's resources and the fact that international students are not eligible for federally funded aid. As of this writing, there are only six colleges in the U.S. that extend need-blind, full-need admissions for both U.S. and international students: Amherst College, Harvard College, MIT, Princeton University, Yale University, and the Minerva Schools at KGI (part of the Claremont University Consortium)—all highly selective schools with very competitive applicant pools. The remainder of the Ivy League is need-blind for U.S. students, need-sensitive for international students, and will meet the full demonstrated need for all accepted students. An additional thirty-three selective schools follow the same policies. Some public universities will consider in-state students under need-blind, full-need policies, but not out-of-state students.

> A need-blind admission policy is most meaningful when it is combined with a commitment from the school to meet every accepted students' demonstrated need.

Survey Says

What's the biggest concern of students and parents about applying to college?

38% say level of debt to pay for the degree

32% say will get into first-choice college, but won't be able to attend due to high cost/insufficient financial aid

23% say won't get into first-choice college

7% say will attend a college I (my child) may not be happy about

*Results of The Princeton Review's 2017 College Hopes & Worries Survey of college applicants and parents of college applicants.

Will I be penalized if I apply for financial aid?
Will colleges looks favorably on me if I don't apply for financial aid?

These two questions are asking the same thing: At colleges and universities that are need-blind, do students who can pay full freight for four years have an edge when it comes to gaining admission? Sometimes. If you are in this fortunate position and your dream school is a highly selective, need-blind university, you might want to confirm that a couple of other schools on your list are need-aware. If you know you will need financial aid to complete your degree and your dream school is need-aware, you might consider adding a need-blind college to your list.

Ultimately, these policies should not play a major role in choosing the colleges that fit you best. Most colleges and universities do not give your finances significant weight in admission decisions. You are better served focusing on the college's academic offerings and extracurricular resources when choosing where to apply, and working on your grades and test scores to increase your chances of acceptance.

Need-aware admission policies also do not provide strategic leverage on your application. The only scenario where the ability to pay for college can meaningfully impact your college decision is if your application lands in the "maybe" pile at a need-aware institution. In that case, being able to pay full sticker price may help move you into the "accepted" category. If you have a lackluster transcript and average test scores, your bank account is not going to get you into college. If you will need financial aid and anticipate that you are eligible for it, you should apply for it and answer any relevant questions on your college application honestly (the Common Application asks if you will be applying for aid or not). If you indicate on your application that you will not need aid and get accepted, you won't be able to apply for financial aid later—the school's financial aid office will have already apportioned the aid available for the year. It doesn't

> The only scenario where the ability to pay for college can meaningfully impact your college decision is if your application lands in the "maybe" pile at a need-aware institution. In that case, being able to pay full sticker price may help move you into the "accepted" category.

matter if you get into a great school if you can't pay for it (and taking on loads of debt to pay for college isn't a great idea for your financial future).

Need-Blind vs Need-Aware Admission	
Need-Blind Admission	An applicant's ability to pay for their education will not be a factor in the college's decision to admit, wait list, or deny the applicant. Need-blind admission doesn't require that an applicant with demonstrated financial need be awarded financial aid, nor does it require that 100 percent of the applicant's demonstrated need be met.
Need-Aware Admission	Colleges do consider an applicant's ability to pay for their education when making admission decisions. This control can allow colleges to meet full need for all accepted students.

Can I appeal my financial aid decision?

Yes, but doing so requires a delicate approach and sound reasoning. If the financial aid package you have received works for your financial situation, you are unlikely to be granted additional funding. Parents, you may pride yourselves on your business negotiation or bargain haggling skills, but you'll find that financial aid officers won't be worn down or tricked into making college tuition a better deal for you. If, however, the package offered by your dream school is prohibitively low, or you are trying to decide between two schools with similar reputations that have offered you different aid packages, it may be worth approaching the financial aid office for a discussion. You won't be risking your initial offer in doing so.

Below, find our tips on appealing your financial aid decision, culled from *Paying for College Without Going Broke*.

1. **Timing is everything.** If you're going to appeal, do so before you've committed to attend any school, and avoid waiting until right before the deadline to do so (usually May 1).

2. **Reach out.** Call the financial aid office or ask for an in-person meeting if you live nearby. You want to do this person to person, not over email. Ask to speak to or meet with the head of the office, if possible.

3. **Get prepped.** Have copies of your FAFSA and other financial aid forms on hand, as well as any other aid offers you are considering.

4. **Be honest.** Any claims you make about your finances or another school's offer must be backed up by documentation.

5. **Be polite.** Aggression or confrontation will not earn you any love from financial aid officers.

Is it a smart move to attend a two year/associates degree granting school first to save money?

> If you plan to begin your degree at one school and graduate from another, it is essential that your pre-transfer grades are excellent.

I've heard more and more questions like this as college costs have increased dramatically in recent years and families are experiencing sticker shock. If your goal is to obtain a bachelor's degree but you're finding that a four-year school seems cost-prohibitive no matter how you crunch the numbers, you might consider starting at a community college or public in-state university and applying to transfer to your dream school after one or two years. The total cost of your degree will be significantly lower than four years of private college. You will be more likely to transfer your credits from another four-year degree program to the school that will ultimately award your degree than from an associate's or two-year program—and, in the event that plans change, you're still on track to a bachelor's degree. (I dive into transfer applications in Chapter 8.)

One caveat: Transferring colleges can be trickier than applying right out of high school. If you plan to begin your degree at one school and graduate from another, it is essential that your pre-transfer grades are excellent. Make sure you leverage every possible resource for academic support, whether that's the university writing center, a professor's office hours, or peer tutoring.

9 Creative Ways to Pay Less for College

1. **Attend a community college for two years and transfer to a pricier school to complete the degree.** Plan ahead: Be sure the college you plan to transfer to will accept the community college credits.

2. **Look into "cooperative education" programs.** Over 900 colleges allow students to combine college education with a job. It can take longer to complete a degree this way. But graduates generally owe less in student loans and have a better chance of getting hired.

3. **Take as many AP courses as possible and get high scores on AP exams.** Many colleges award course credits for high AP scores. Some students have cut a year off their college tuition this way.

4. **Earn college credit via "dual enrollment" programs available at some high schools.** These allow students to take college level courses during their senior year.

5. **Earn college credits by taking CLEP (College-Level Examination Program) exams.** Depending on the college, a qualifying score on any of the thirty-three CLEP exams can earn students three to twelve college credits. (See Princeton Review's *Cracking the CLEP*®, 5th Edition.)

6. **Stick to your college and your major.** Changing colleges can result in lost credits. Aid may be limited/not available for transfer students at some schools. Changing majors can mean paying for extra courses to meet requirements.

7. **Finish college in three years if possible.** Take the maximum number of credits every semester, attend summer sessions, and earn credits via online courses. Some colleges offer three-year programs for high-achieving students.

8. **Let Uncle Sam pay for your degree.** ROTC (Reserve Officer Training Corps) programs available from U.S. Armed Forces branches (except the Coast Guard) offer merit-based scholarships up to full tuition via participating colleges in exchange for military service after you graduate.

9. **Better yet:** Attend a tuition-free college.

*From *Paying for College Without Going Broke*, 2018 Edition by Kalman Chany

Chapter 6

Application

CHAPTER 6
Application

To become a competitive college applicant, you have three jobs to do while you're in high school:

1. Be awesome academically and take on a challenging work load.

2. Do well on standardized tests.

3. Research colleges to equip yourself with as much information as possible.

Of course, there's still one more activity you'll need to complete if you want to go to college: the actual process of applying to college.

What is the Common Application?

The Common Application is an online app that you can use to submit your information to multiple schools. Over 700 colleges and universities accept the Common App. While different schools often use different essay prompts or ask you to answer additional questions in shorter form, all schools need your contact details, the name of your high school, a list of your extracurricular activities, some information about your family, and so on. Having a tool that allows you to create a profile of this information that you can send to most, if not all, of the schools on your list is a major time saver. When I applied to college, we had to enter the same information about ourselves over and over on paper forms by hand! The Common App also makes it easy to keep track of which documents you've completed and submitted to each school.

The Common App is updated for each academic year on August 1. You can create an account at commonapp.org. Be sure to confirm each school's specific admission requirements, like the number of recommendation letters you'll need, SAT Subject Test minimums, and school-specific forms or essays, as well.

4 Tips for Managing College Application Stress (from Real Students Who Have Been There)

1. **Mark everything on a calendar.** "Create a schedule for application and scholarship deadlines and prioritize by the due dates."

2. **Be open-minded.** "College is about finding your happiness, not your parents' happiness or what would look good on your bumper."

3. **Keep the end goal in mind.** "Don't get frustrated with applications. Just think of how good you'll feel in the fall walking the halls of your chosen college."

4. **Ask questions.** "Guidance counselors, your parents, and your friends are there for you to help with your stress levels and the college decision process. While you may feel alone with your emotions over college, the people you are surrounded with have probably felt the same way you do now."

*Results of The Princeton Review's 2017 College Hopes & Worries Survey

Are there other applications like the Common Application? Is one better than another?

There are a few similar application options for smaller cohorts of schools, as well. ApplyTexas is an application system for public universities and many other institutions in Texas; California uses one system for all the University of California schools and another system for all Cal State University schools. There is also an alternative to the Common App called the Coalition Application that is accepted by 113 colleges and universities. The information on the Coalition App will be substantively similar to what is collected on the Common App, but the digital interface is different. The Coalition Application makes it simple to apply for application fee waivers and provides online tools you can use to share your application materials for feedback with your teachers and counselors.

Some colleges use one application type exclusively. Others may accept either the Common Application or the Coalition Application and might have a proprietary application in the mix, too. If a school accepts more than one type of application, you should choose the option that works best for you—admission officers do not prefer one over the other.

> If a school accepts more than one type of application, you should choose the option that works best for you—admission officers do not prefer one over the other.

4 Types of College Applications

	What is it	School examples:
The Common Application	A single online college application form used by over 700 colleges and universities.	• Stanford University • The College of William & Mary
Coalition Application	A single online college application and digital portfolio used by the 113 member schools of the Coalition for Access, Affordability, and Success.	• University of Pennsylvania • Yale University
Universal College Application	A single online college application used by 23 colleges and universities.	• Harvard College • Johns Hopkins University
College-Specific Applications	Many university systems or schools have their own exclusive application.	• University of California (UC Application) • University of Texas (ApplyTexas)

Note: Many colleges accept more than one type of application. For example, Harvard College accepts the Common Application, the Universal College Application, or the Coalition Application.

What do admission officers look for in an application essay?

First and foremost, application readers want to know that you can write. That doesn't mean you need to use a lot of big words or flowery metaphors. Your sentences should be clear, your ideas organized and logical, and your grammar, punctuation, and spelling should be flawless. Patience, revision, and proofreading will help you refine these aspects of your essay. Start writing early and give yourself time to work through a few drafts.

What to write about is another matter, and one of the more overwhelming and anxiety-inducing aspects of the admission process. Most schools that require essays will provide a writing prompt, or a few prompts to choose from, but many of the prompts or questions used are open-ended enough that you can write about almost anything. Choose something that is important to you and will give you opportunities to tell admission officers about yourself. You should be able to explain why the topic or experience matters to you and how it has influenced you.

It's also important that your voice comes through in your essay. You don't need to be overly ambitious with your writing style or form, and a tone that feels affected or inauthentic may work against you. Think about how you would tell the story of your essay in a face-to-face interview. When you write with language that doesn't come naturally to you, it shows, and your essay may feel strained and miss the mark.

YOU should write your essay, not your older sibling or a parent or private admission counselor. That said, you will want to solicit feedback and proofreads from one or two adults whose opinions you trust. Getting feedback on your work will help you craft a stronger essay, and extra eyes will help you catch typos. Don't go overboard with input, though—too many conflicting opinions and suggestions can make you doubt your instincts and result in a flat essay that feels written-by-committee.

If you are applying to several schools, be very careful when re-using essays on different applications. You may need to make small tweaks to your main essay for each school. Make sure the essays you're submitting are responses to the school's prompts, and ALWAYS double check any school names in your essays or short answers—many, many admission officers have told me about receiving essays in which the applicant has left in a mention of another college. That's a fast track to the rejection pile.

5 Tips for College Essays

1. **Tell the story that grades and test scores can't capture.** A thoughtful and sincere essay about something that's important to you—an experience, a person, or even a book—shows colleges the unique qualities you will add to the incoming class.

2. **Always be yourself in your application, not the candidate you think admission committees want to see.** Sometimes it's better to write about an experience that was hard for you because you learned something than it is to write about something that was easy for you because you think it sounds impressive.

3. **Remember to reflect.** You're not the only applicant to win the class presidency, go on a service trip, or suffer an athletic injury. Take the opportunity to really examine how an experience taught you something you didn't previously know about yourself, got you out of your comfort zone, or forced you to grow.

4. **Start early, and write several drafts.** Coming up with an original, thoughtful essay topic will inevitably take a fair amount of brainstorming. Make sure you start writing early in the application process.

5. **Ask a parent, teacher, or friend you trust to be your editor.** The more time you spend with a piece of your own writing, the less likely you are to spot errors (and your college essays must be 100 percent typo free!).

When should I start the application process?

Ideally, you should be thinking about college throughout high school, choosing courses and extracurriculars that will set you up to be a competitive applicant, researching and visiting schools in your junior year, and preparing for the SAT and/or ACT before the start of your senior year.

As for completing the application itself, my advice has always been to start early, and this has been echoed by many parents and students on our annual "College Hopes & Worries" survey over the years. The more time you give yourself to craft a strong application, the less stressed out you will feel, and the more options you will have if something goes unexpectedly off the rails. If you are completing the Common Application, you can start working on it as early as August 1st (Note: Last year, the Common App announced its new essay prompts for the upcoming academic year in February, so you can start drafting your essays even earlier). If you are applying for financial aid, you will be able to start the FAFSA as early as October 1. College application deadlines vary, but typically Early Decision deadlines fall in early November and Regular deadlines fall in early January. If any of the colleges on your list have rolling admissions, applying as early as possible can help give your application a boost. Rolling admission means that applications are accepted over a few months, and admissions decisions are made as applications are received, instead of all at once following a cut-off date. So, there are a lot more spots open at those schools early in the application timeframe than there will be closer to their final deadline.

> The more time you give yourself to craft a strong application, the less stressed out you will feel, and the more options you will have if something goes unexpectedly off the rails.

Another good reason to begin preparing your application materials early is that you will need to rely on other folks or systems to obtain some materials, and this can take a bit of time. Your high school is processing requests for academic transcripts for all your peers applying to college at the same time, so confirming that your transcripts have been sent may take a few days or weeks. If you have concerns about your standardized test scores, you may want additional time to prep for and retake the SAT and/or ACT, and like transcripts your official score reports will take a few weeks to reach the colleges where you're applying. Once you've completed the FAFSA, and the CSS PROFILE if necessary, the official analysis of your financial information can take up to four weeks before it is provided to your schools. And don't forget about letters of recommendation: you should give your letter-writers at least a month to draft and submit your recommendations, especially if you know they are writing recs for many other applicants.

College Essay Advice (from a Real Student Who Has Been There)

"Once the Common Application or specific college applications open, look over the essay questions and requirements. Begin gathering ideas and outlines for them over the summer after Junior Year. Have rough drafts as early as possible to begin editing and accommodating the word counts."

—2017 College Hopes & Worries Survey

Parent to Parent

College to Career

"We pick schools in an upside down fashion. We pick a school based on reputation, then find a major we think we might like, and then four years later try to shoehorn a career around it.

The better way—Determine the career, understand which major will best lead to that career, then find the school that does the best job for that major / career."

—2017 College Hopes & Worries Survey

Should I declare a major on my application or apply undecided?

Unless you are applying to a specific school within a university or unique program dedicated to an academic track, you do not need to declare a major on your college application. If you do inform the admissions office of what you'd like to study, no one will hold you to that later if you change your mind. In most liberal arts academic programs, students must declare a major by the end of sophomore year. If you don't know what major to choose, you'll have time to evaluate the different academic offerings (and work towards any general education requirements) at your school during your first two years, and you'll spend your junior and senior year focusing on the requirements for your major.

It's common for parents and applicants to believe that declaring a major on a college application matters in the admission decision. Some people think that declaring a major shows focus and passion, and helps to communicate what you will bring to the campus community. Some people worry that admission officers have quotas for different majors and committing to something popular like English may work against them if many other students have chosen the same major. In most cases, admission officers do not expect the majority of high school seniors to have their careers mapped out, nor will they penalize you if you know what you want to study. If you must declare a major on your application and it will be considered inside the admissions office, the school will make that clear.

If you do know what you want to study, go ahead and include that in your application. The more information admission officers have about you, the clearer it will be that you're a great fit for their school.

College Major Advice
(from a Real Student Who Has Been There)

"Still go to college even if you do not know what you want to study. Don't let the unknown scare you because you might find out your passion in college."

—2017 College Hopes & Worries Survey

How important is optional or supplementary application material?

It's right there in the name: optional or supplemental.

If you don't submit any additional information or achievements outside the required application materials, the lack thereof won't work against you.

If you don't submit any additional information or achievements outside the required application materials, the lack thereof won't work against you. If you have not found a place in your application to share an interest, pursuit, or accomplishment, this is your chance to do so—it never hurts you to provide admission officers with additional information on your strengths and skills.

Optional or supplemental application material is a great way to share something visual with admission officers, like an art portfolio, a video of a theatrical performance, or debate team competition. Visual media has the additional value of helping you stand out in both the applicant pool and an admission officer's mind.

You don't need to leverage optional/supplemental material for anything that would be redundant with other parts of your application. If you're required to submit an academic writing sample with your application, you don't need to submit a second sample here. If you've won academic awards or athletic competitions and these are listed on your application or appear in your essay, there's little benefit in re-confirming these achievements here. Admission officers are incredibly busy during application season, and most aren't able to give optional/supplemental material more time and attention than the average application receives. If your application is a complete and accurate picture of you, you've done a great job and don't need to add anything additional. If you do want to submit additional material, make sure that it's adding something to your application, that it can be understood quickly by busy admission officers, and that you follow the school's directions for submitting material to a T.

Is a college interview required? What should I expect?

Interview requirements differ from school to school. Many colleges and universities offer applicants the opportunity to interview on campus with a member of the admissions team, or locally with an alumnus/ae who has been trained to do so. Often interviews are optional or encouraged rather than required. If you are able to interview, whether it's required or not, I recommend that you do! This is another opportunity to make an impression on the admissions committee (especially if you're able to interview with a staff member on campus) and share what you can uniquely bring to campus.

A college interview is also helpful for you to make sure the school where you're applying is a good fit for you. Your interviewer is representing the campus community, so if you connect with them, that's a good sign. It's also an awesome opportunity to ask in-depth questions about the school that you haven't been able to answer in your research. Not only will you get some info that you want, but you'll show the interviewer that you're invested in attending the school, curious, and informed. Try to avoid asking generic questions or questions that you could easily answer online.

Be specific when you talk about your interest in the school. Why does it feel like a good fit for you? What about it stood out when you were visiting or researching? Alumni who conduct admission interviews are typically people who valued their college experience and remain involved with the community—they love their alma maters, and they want to know that you will, too.

With any interview, you should prepare for commonly asked questions, and try to practice with a parent, teacher, or counselor to make sure you know your talking points and feel comfortable adapting if you get a question you're not expecting. You want to present yourself as confident and comfortable, but also professional and poised. If you've interviewed before for a job or internship, you have valuable experience. If you haven't yet, your college admissions interview will be a valuable learning experience you can draw on in future job interviews.

Interview Tips
(From Real Students Who Have Been There)

Don't just take my word for it. Here are some smart tips from last year's crop of college applicants.

1. **Interviewers know sincere enthusiasm when they see it.** "Before you apply to any college, learn about all the reasons that make you want to go there. This really helps as not only will this be used in the interviews but also in your application; your application must talk about you, and how you see yourself in the college."

2. **Take advantage of interview opportunities.** "If the college you're interested in offers it, do take the time to do an on-campus or off-campus interview. Register for the visits and tours early because those fill up fast especially in the months of September, October, and November."

3. **Politeness pays off.** "Always send 'thank you' notes."

4. **Be true to you.** "Colleges want to know how you are as a person, so in interviews and such, just be yourself! Show them your awesome identity!"

5. **Show them you're serious.** "If you are really interested in a college, let them know! Request an informal alumni interview before interviewing with an admissions counselor."

6. **Knowing you're prepared will help you relax.** "Take many deep breaths. Practice and go into interviews with confidence!"

*Results of The Princeton Review's 2017 College Hopes & Worries Survey

College Interview FAQs

If you're ready to discuss these seven topics, you'll be ready for your college interview.

1. What's an example of a challenge that you overcame, and what did you learn from it?

2. What's your favorite high school class and why?

3. Tell me something about you that I wouldn't know from your application.

4. What do you plan to study in college? (Hint: if you're undeclared, that's totally okay—this question gives you an opportunity talk about different majors or careers you are considering, and how you might go about choosing a major if you're accepted.)

5. Why do you want to attend this college or university?

6. What do you enjoy doing when you're not in class?

7. Do you have any questions for ME?

Who should I ask to write my letters of recommendation?

While your grades, test scores, and transcript will always be the most crucial parts of your application, letters of recommendation are very important. These letters represent professional adults, usually teachers and guidance counselors, who are endorsing your academic performance and your future plans. You will probably need at least two letters of recommendation from teachers you've had for academic subjects (as opposed to electives), though some schools ask for three recommendations or offer you the option of submitting additional letters of support from coaches, employers, or counselors. These recommendations are submitted directly to the school—you won't get to see them before the admission officers do.

You will want to choose your recommenders wisely; you don't have to ask the teachers who gave you the best grades. In fact, a teacher who has seen you face challenges and has supported your growth would be in a terrific position to write you a recommendation. You should choose teachers with whom you have a connection and who are familiar with your academic track record. If you're unsure who to ask for recommendation letters, you should talk through your options with a parent or your high school guidance counselor. If you're reading this book in 9th or 10th grade, think about how you might build relationships with teachers you like. Look for opportunities to ask for extra help or work with the teacher outside of class, and think about your class participation. Do you have a lot to say in class? How does the teacher respond? You'll want to build similar relationships with your college professors and eventually with work superiors, so this is a skillset that you will use throughout your life.

Plan ahead and approach these tasks professionally. Chances are you are not the only student asking for a recommendation letter during application season, so be sure to give your recommenders enough time to draft and submit your letters before the deadline. They will either need to mail signed hard copies or use online tools to securely submit their letters (both the Common App and Coalition App have options for submitting recommendation letters online). When you ask your teachers to write you recommendations, you should have any materials (forms, addressed stamped envelopes), deadlines, URLs, and submission instructions they will need to submit letters on time. I recommend that you also offer a list of extracurricular activities, a draft of your college essay, and any other info that you think might be relevant. This will help give your teacher fodder for their letter and put their recommendation into the full context of your application. It's especially helpful if you're approaching a teacher you had before senior year—you can update them on your latest accomplishments. Finally, don't forget to be polite when you ask for letters, and send a thank you note for the letter once you've submitted your application. It's poor form to wait until you're accepted by the college to say thank you, but you should absolutely let your recommenders know when and where you get in—they're invested in your admission process, too.

How to Ask for Letters of Recommendation

Stumbling up to a teacher at the end of class, dumping paperwork on his desk and asking if the teacher can write a letter of recommendation for an application that's due in two weeks? Not good.

1. **Check with your high school counselor first.** Some high schools have established systems they want their students to follow for requesting letters of recommendation.

2. **Ask early.** Preferably as early as possible in your senior year or even in your junior year (once you have the necessary materials).

3. **Get detailed.** Give your teacher some indication of why you are asking them in particular. I recommend giving your teacher a list of your extracurricular activities, a draft of your application essay, and any other information you think is important so they have ideas for what to write in the letter.

4. **Be exceedingly polite.** Remember: you're basically assigning your teachers homework. Above all else, be kind and considerate when interacting with your teacher.

5. **Send your teachers each college's specific instructions and deadlines.** You may need to fill out a form from the college, provide credentials and information for a college's online application system, or get an addressed and stamped envelope.

8 Questions to Ask Your High School Counselor

Your high school counselor is your #1 resource for college prep and applications. Here are some questions to kick off the process.

1. What's the right high school schedule for me?

2. Am I on track for graduation requirements?

3. Are any colleges visiting our high school this year?

4. What are some appropriate colleges for me to look at?

5. What extracurricular activities can I get involved with?

6. What do I need to fill out the FAFSA?

7. Can you help me find local scholarships?

8. Do you have any special instructions for students requesting transcripts, counselor reports, or letters of recommendation?

Chapter 7

Inside the Admission Office

Inside the Admission Office

In this chapter, we take a look behind the curtain at what goes on inside a college admission office. You've hit send on your application, your transcripts and scores have been all been mailed—now what? Let's investigate the review process, including who is actually reading your application, how they make a decision, and next steps you can take after an admissions roadblock like deferred admission or getting waitlisted.

What are my chances of getting into my dream school?

To honestly assess your chances at getting into a college, you need to find out how you stack up to the students who go there. Carefully research each college's admission standards and compare your GPA, SAT and/or ACT scores, class rank, and high school courses to see if schools you are considering are a good academic fit. Colleges publish averages for their most recently accepted first-year class on their websites, and you can also find these stats in the college profiles on PrincetonReview.com.

> To honestly assess your chances at getting into a college, you need to find out how you stack up to the students who go there.

You'll also want to check out the school's acceptance rate, which will put those other numbers (GPA, test scores, etc.) into perspective:

- If the acceptance rate of a school is at least 50 percent, and your GPA and test scores are about the same as the middle range for the first-year class, you can consider that a "target school." It's not a guarantee you'll get in, but the odds seem to be in your favor.

- If the acceptance rate of a school is between 35 to 45 percent, your grades and test scores would need to be near the high end of the range to consider that a target school.

- Any college that accepts fewer than 20 percent of the applicants is a highly selective school and usually a reach for just about everybody.

This isn't an exact science, as many of these schools will also be looking at activities, letters of recommendation, essays and your interview, all of which can influence a decision.

But what is a dream school anyway? If you mean that, based on all of your research, your dream school is your best-fit school academically, campus culturally, as well as financially and from a career services perspective, then your chances of earning admission should be excellent for the simple fact that you've done your homework.

That's really the ideal—finding a place where you say "YES, that's the school for me!" and "YES, that's the place that suits me best!" Sometimes, it's easier said than done as you might imagine. Sometimes it's easy to get wowed by a school's brand name and the perception that a school in and of itself is going to guarantee you an awesome and successful future.

The truth is that no school can ever make that guarantee, but you have the ability to earn those lofty levels of success at any school you choose. It sounds simple, and it is. Provided you do the digging and the honest research through that best-fit lens and resist being overwhelmed by brand or raw admission difficulty as the only definition of a dream school then you're going to do oh so well!

On Dealing with Rejection (from A Real Student Who Has Been There)

"There is a place for everyone. Relax and think of it as a journey—not a race to be won, but a home to be found."

—2017 College Hopes & Worries Survey

How are my application materials reviewed?

What does go on behind closed doors once your application reaches the admissions office? The answer is not so simple because colleges and universities use their own formulas. At some schools, the evaluation is an exercise in number-crunching. If you've taken the required classes, cleared the minimum GPA and earned the minimum tests scores, you're in. Other schools undergo a more personal evaluation. They use your application to get a sense of who you are beyond the numbers and how you might contribute on campus.

Here's an example of how it can work at selective colleges (schools that admit fewer than 75 percent of their applicants):

Student's applications are handed off to an admissions officer ("a reader") for a preliminary reading. Most readers start by reviewing the rigor of your classes, the grades you've earned, and your test scores. They'll look through your essays, read your letters of recommendation, peruse your extracurriculars, and consult your interviewer's report. During this time, readers may take notes on each part of the application, and write a summary of your strengths and weaknesses and anything else that was compelling or interesting about you.

At many schools, if you're clearly admissible (meaning your high school GPA and standardized test scores, etc. sit well within or above the mean for accepted students at that school), then the decision to admit you might well rely on the positive recommendation of that first reader. The recommendation can be reviewed by others on the admission team, but basically, you've cleared the first major hurdle!

Same drill on the other end of the spectrum, if your high school GPA, standardized test scores, etc. are well below the mean, then the admission officer making the initial recommendation to deny your application will likely stick.

If you make it past the first reader, it's possible that a second reader may weigh in and compare their impressions with those of the first reader. Some applications may be accepted right then if both readers agree on the application, some may be sent to another senior admissions officer to review, and some may be sent to the larger committee for discussion.

5 Reasons to Take BOTH the SAT and ACT

1. **Give more information to the admissions committee.** Some of the most selective schools are reporting that as much as a quarter or more of their enrolled students submitted scores for both exams.

2. **Prep more efficiently.** Plan to take both tests and you'll be able to make an informed decision about which one best displays your strengths.

3. **Increase your chances of receiving merit aid.** Even if the college or university you're applying to doesn't require test scores for admission, ACT or SAT scores may be required to be considered for merit-based financial aid and any outside scholarship applications.

4. **Take fewer tests (no, really!).** Some schools require applicants to submit scores from the ACT or the SAT plus two to three SAT Subject tests. If you plan on taking the SAT, take the ACT too so you're covered in case something goes wrong on one of your SAT Subject Tests.

5. **Multiply your options.** When it comes to choosing test dates, considering both tests gives you more flexibility.

If your application makes it to this point, at least one of the admission officers wants to admit you! But all of the other admissions officers have applicants they want to admit, too, and at selective colleges, they can't admit everybody. Your admissions officers will plead your case by summarizing the most compelling parts of your application—anything from your riveting application essay to a single line in a recommendation letter that makes them think you will thrive at their college. They'll fight for you.

Of course, different schools will use different variations of the system described above, but here's one constant. Real humans will evaluate you. When they do, they'll look at lots of things beyond just grades and test scores.

What Do Application Readers Look For?

1. Grades

Did you challenge yourself with honors classes, AP classes, and IB classes when they were available?

Grades matter all four years. When colleges review your transcript, they typically focus on your sophomore and junior year grades but will still see the others. Many schools will reward an upward trajectory!

2. Test Scores

SAT and ACT scores take the lead, but admissions officers consider your performance on AP exams and SAT Subject Tests as well.

Even at test optional schools, your standardized test scores can qualify you for merit scholarships.

3. Letters of Recommendation

Readers are looking for descriptions and anecdotes that show off your unique personality and interests.

Typically applications will ask for letters of recommendation from at least two teachers, but some may allow you to include additional notes from coaches, employers, or counselors.

4. Extracurriculars

What you do with your time outside the classroom shows colleges who you are and what qualities you'll bring to campus.

Commitment to a sport, hobby, religious organization, or job over four years of high school is key. Colleges would much rather see you excited about a few worthwhile endeavors than marginally involved with a ton of clubs.

5. Application Essay

What's your story? What's important to you?

You don't need to have started your own business or have spent the summer hiking the Appalachian Trail. Colleges are simply looking for thoughtful, motivated students who will add something to the first-year class.

Who is on the admission committee?

As the name implies, your admission decision doesn't rest on the whim of just one person, but likely in the hands of many. What a relief, right? It's good to remind ourselves that the admission review process is a VERY HUMAN process at lots and lots of schools.

Admission committees are comprised of the admission officers responsible for reading and evaluating applications from your high school (and other high schools in your state, region of the country, etc.). It's common for colleges to group applications by geographic region so that each reader is evaluating students from a particular territory, allowing readers to get familiar with the high schools in their assigned areas.

Of course, different colleges have different systems. At some, undergraduates and faculty members play a role. At others, all decisions are made by a small handful of professionals. At still others, decisions are made democratically by large committees. Depending on the size of the college, a school's Director of Admission, Dean of Admission, Vice President of Enrollment (and other top brass) may all weigh in on your application. Suffice it to say, that lots more than just one person will be evaluating your application. Since the admission process can be so subjective—both for applicants and admission officers—that's such a good thing!

What is the single most important thing admission officers look for in an application?

The #1 most important piece of information that a student will submit on their college application is universal to all schools (public, private, large, small, etc.). The answer is your high school GPA/high school transcript. OK, it's a pork-bellied answer as that's clearly two different things. But, they're oh so related!

> You can never underestimate the power and raw heft of your high school transcript and GPA.

Going forth after reading this answer you can never underestimate the power and raw heft of your high school transcript and GPA. Your high school transcript is the weightiest of documents in your application because it's a complete record of your academic achievements in four years of high school. The document contains your cumulative GPA for all four years, but also the classes you took and the grades you received in each of those classes. Most importantly, your transcript answers this question, "Have you consistently challenged yourself academically throughout high school?" Have you challenged yourself with regular courses? Honors classes? APs? IBs? No, this doesn't mean you have to take every single Advanced Placement class, or that you can never take a fun and easy elective (not that there's anything easy about ballroom dancing, trust me). However, admission counselors are looking for evidence that you're willing to undertake challenging coursework on a consistent basis—evidence that you'll do well in college. Never underestimate the importance of your high school transcript to the college admission process.

Of course, just signing up for impressive classes won't cut the mustard—you'll have to do well in these courses, too. While it's true that it looks better to take difficult classes and not always get sky high grades than to take easy classes and always excel, a high overall GPA is crucial. What to do if you have poor grades? It's time to light a fire under them and heat them up. Don't think that just because your grades are low everything's lost. Most college admission offices look favorably on students who start off poorly but then work to raise their grades.

I suspect you're wondering about what the second most important piece of information that you'll submit with your application might be. This one does waiver a bit from school to school, but it's still solidly the second most reported important piece of info. The answer is standardized test scores—the SAT and ACT being the most important.

How to Evaluate Your Admissions Chances

1. **Research the college's most recent first-year class.** Search for your college on PrincetonReview.com/college-search (or find the "Class Profile" on the college's own website).

2. **Know what stats to look for.** Find these pieces of information about the college's current first-year class:

   • The SAT/ACT range for the middle 50 percent

   • The average high school GPA

   • How many freshmen were in the top 10, 25, 50, etc. percent of their high school class

   • The overall percentage of applicants accepted.

3. **Interpret the data.** The acceptance rate of a college gives you an idea of where your GPA and test scores need to be to have a good chance of admission.

Will applying Early Decision or Early Action give me a leg up?

I so want to give you a direct and universal answer to this question, but it's not so straightforward. The truth: the answer varies from school to school. That said, the broad-brush strokes I go into below will keep things in some perspective.

But first, let's dig into the terminology.

Many colleges allow applicants to submit their materials for an early deadline (sometime in the fall) that falls before the regular deadline (usually sometime in January or February).

> **Early Decision** is binding. This means if you are accepted through early decision, you are committed to attending that school, and will withdraw any applications you may have submitted for the regular deadlines at other schools. You may not apply to more than one college under early decision. If you are not accepted, you will either be rejected or deferred. Rejected applicants may not apply again that year. Deferred applicants will be reconsidered during the regular admission period, and are free to apply to other schools (More about deferred admission coming up). Early decision deadlines are often in November, and students are typically notified of the decision in December.

> **Early Action** is non–binding. This means you are not bound to attend if you are accepted. You may also apply early action to multiple colleges. Early action deadlines usually fall at the same time as early decision.

Early Admission Strategies

Most early decision schools (that is, schools that offer an early decision admission option) admit between 10 to 20 percent of their incoming freshman classes as early decision. Hence, the majority of students are admitted through the regular decision channel.

However, there is an increasing number of early decision schools (many offering Early Decision 1 and Early Decision 2 deadline alternatives) which admit 30 to 45 percent of their freshman classes early decision! At those kinds of schools, it makes it harder for students to be admitted through the regular decision channel. Early decision could offer a leg-up at such schools.

Early action has all the value of early decision but few of the obligations. That's attractive from a student perspective (general sigh of relief) but offers little from the admission strategy perspective. The obvious advantage of early action over early decision is the opportunity it gives you to apply to, and ultimately compare financial aid packages from several schools. If you are accepted early decision, you risk missing the admission deadlines of other schools while you wait for your award package to arrive. If that award is lackluster, your options are fewer.

If you're sure that you've found your best-fit school, you know it's one you want to attend, you're a strong candidate for admission, and you know that you can afford the tuition, go ahead and apply early decision.

That is a whole lot of research and comparison to have done by fall of your senior year, though, and if you're uncertain about any of those factors, you're not alone! Keep your options open by applying early action, or by the regular deadline.

College Admission Options

Application Type	*Deadline	Is the decision binding?	If you're accepted, when do you decide?
Regular Admissions	On or around January 1	No	May 1
Rolling Admissions	Within the school's "application window," usually a 6-month period between August and March	No	May 1
Early Decision	November 1 or 15	Yes	N/A. Early decision is binding. If you're accepted, you're going!
Early Action	November 1 or 15	No	May 1

*ALWAYS double-check deadlines with each of your prospective schools. The deadlines listed here are approximates.

What does it mean to be deferred? What can I do to improve my chances of acceptance?

First off, being deferred doesn't mean that you've been denied. Generally, students receive deferrals if they've applied to a school through early decision or early action channels. If a school doesn't admit a student outright through those early channels (most don't) your application moves to (is "deferred to") the regular decision channel.

In my book, a deferral to that regular admission channel means opportunity! You're done with the hard work, and your application is already in the regular admission pool at your first-choice college. So, take heart. A deferral is an indication that the admission committee thinks your qualifications are solid. They are just getting a sense of the full applicant pool for the year. That same admission committee will review your application in full (again) in roughly two-months time.

Deferred? Here's what to do.

- If you haven't visited the school in person or haven't had an admission interview (should a school offer them) then do it! Nothing screams "I'm serious about your school!" like showing up in person.

- Remember that admission counselors reviewing your application in the regular decision channel will be reviewing your newest high school marking period grades and any new standardized test scores. Your academic awesomeness will have a chance to shine yet again!

- Here's another way to be proactive. In late January or early February, compose a letter or email to the school and ask that it be included with your application materials. The letter should provide an update on your activities since the early application deadline. Include your first semester grades and any academic highlights, new developments in your extracurricular activities, and your plans for the rest of senior year. Request an interview if you haven't had one yet. Then, reiterate your undying love for this school above all others, all the reasons why you are a great fit, and your commitment to enroll if admitted.

- Full steam ahead (with regular decision applications, that is). Remain optimistic, but create your contingency plan. You already have the foundation of a great college application. You probably already have a list of schools that you considered on your way to choosing where to submit that early application. Revisit that list. Does it include schools that suit your interests and goals? Schools you can afford to attend? Schools where you're likely to gain admittance? Prepare applications for regular decision deadlines with the same attention to detail you invested in your early application, and submit them on time. Hold out hope that you get into your top choice, but aim for acceptance at a few other schools, so you have some to choose from in the spring.

What are my chances of getting off the waitlist?

I'm such a glass half full kinda guy, but I would be dishonest if I told you the chances were good. Nationally, relatively few applicants placed on a waitlist earn academic admission.

But first, let's make sure we're all on the same page about what a waitlist actually is. All selective colleges admit more students than they have room for. They do this because they know that many of the students they admit won't actually enroll. Guessing how many students will enroll is a very inexact science. To protect themselves, most colleges have a wait list. An applicant who is "waitlisted" is one who may be admitted if enough students decide to go somewhere else.

If you're waitlisted at a school you want to attend, there are some things you can do that can help your case substantially. Write a letter or e-mail reaffirming your desire to attend the school. Ask your college counselor to call the admission office. Send a letter describing any honors you've won and other achievements since you sent in your application. When colleges admit students from the waitlist, they almost always give preference to students who make it crystal clear that they really want to attend.

At the most selective schools, admissions from waitlists are sometimes few and far between. Harvard College, for example admitted zero students from the waiting list for the admitted class of 2021. Yale University admitted nineteen waitlisted students and Stanford University admitted fifty-five. We're all human and should recognize that it's a tough thing to reconcile in our heads. Here's the silver lining, though. If you curate a list of schools to which you'll apply (six to eight is the average number of applications submitted by individual students), then you need to be sure that you'd be thrilled (really, I mean it, THRILLED) to attend any one of them if admitted.

Do admission officers look at prospective students' social media accounts?

This answer is so easy. YES, so scrub them. Basically, anything out there in the public square that you've penned, snapped, chirped—essentially anything you've created— is all fair game to be considered and used as evaluation fodder by admission teams at schools large and small.

Want to shine online? Here are some ways to use social media to your advantage.

- Create a LinkedIn profile. Joining this professional network demonstrates you're serious about your future. Make a point to connect with teachers, employers, your parents' friends and colleagues, and others who know you. You could even direct admission teams to your LinkedIn profile by including the address in your application.

- Follow the Twitter, Instagram and Facebook pages of your target schools. This is a great way to learn more about prospective colleges. Plus, by commenting and asking great questions you can raise your name recognition and improve your digital footprint.

- Post your successes on your social media sites just in case someone from admissions takes a peek. Link to the editorial you've written for your school paper, upload a video of your cello recital, or post a photo of your soccer team after a big win. Share articles that underscore your interest in history or your love of modern dance.

> Follow the Twitter, Instagram and Facebook pages of your target schools.

If you're not thrilled with what shows up about you online, there are ways to fix it. Social media accounts are usually some of the top returns, so cleaning up those profiles goes a long way. School activity is likely to show high up as well from writing an article for the school paper to participating in an extracurricular activity or club that's on the high school website. Try starting your own foodie blog or commenting on online news stories from your local paper or even the *New York Times* to boost your online presence.

Just make sure your comments are positive.

The bottom line is that social media is yet another opportunity to show colleges who you really are beyond grades and test scores. While colleges may not officially evaluate your Twitter feed as part of the decision process, you have to assume that a curious admissions officer could take a look.

How to E-mail College Admission Officers

Check out my top tips for communicating with admission officers efficiently and effectively:

1. **Keep it short! Focus on your questions, not on yourself.** This is not the time to tell them how great you are.

2. **Minimize the number of questions you ask.** Make sure the answers to your questions aren't easily accessible on the school's website.

3. **Introduce yourself.** Give your name, high school graduation year, name and city of your high school either in the body of the e-mail or as an e-mail signature.

4. **Check for spelling and grammatical mistakes.** Then check again. And then one more time.

5. **Be professional.** If your e-mail address is anything other than a form of your name or initials, consider creating a new one for college correspondence.

Chapter 8

8

Etc.

Etc.

These questions don't fit nicely into a tidy chapter, but I am asked them all the time. From the admission process for international students to maintaining your sanity during college admission season, here's everything (else) you need to know.

Is the admission process different for international students?

The admission process is a little different for international students, yes.

For one, most U.S. universities require international students to submit scores from an English language proficiency exam, like the TOEFL (Test of English as a Foreign Language) or IELTS (International English Language Testing System). Admission officers want to know that you can succeed in courses delivered in English, even if English is not your first language and if your education was not in English. This also means that many schools place a greater importance on the college essay, another demonstration of English skills.

Otherwise, the factors for admission decisions are largely the same as those for domestic students: grades, test scores, and the strength of your high school curriculum. (For a refresher on crafting competitive applications, refer back to Chapter 7.)

The admit rate for international applicants is a bit lower than the overall admit rate, and the field can be competitive. According to NACAC's 2017 *State of College Admission* report[1], the international student admit rate is 55 percent while the admit rate for first-time freshman students is 66 percent. Of course, the acceptance rate for international

> The admit rate for international applicants is a bit lower than the overall admit rate, and the field can be competitive.

applicants will vary school-by-school and can be much lower, especially at public universities. Do your research before you apply!

School	Total undergraduate enrollment	% international students in student body	# foreign countries represented
University of Pennsylvania	10,019	12.12%	126
Harvard College	6,712	11.61%	100
Massachusetts Institute of Technology	4,524	9.53%	108
University of Michigan—Ann Arbor	28,983	6.82%	88
Virginia Tech	25,791	5.83%	116
University of Georgia	27,951	1.68%	124

*Data reported to The Princeton Review by the school in spring 2016

1   https://www.nacacnet.org/news--publications/publications/state-of-college-admission/

Financial Aid for International Students

You should also keep in mind that for students who are not U.S. citizens or eligible non-citizens, financial aid possibilities are limited. No federal aid, for example, is given to nonresident aliens although schools are free to give out their own grants and scholarships. It's possible that financial aid may not be available for international students through the universities you are considering (this depends on the college).

Check with all the schools on your list to find out what their filing requirements are for international students. Many colleges will ask that you complete special aid forms designed specifically for international students. Some of these colleges will also require a Certificate of Finance, which is issued by the family's bank and details the sources and amounts of funds available to the international applicant.

How difficult is transferring between colleges?

Plenty of students transfer between colleges every year. In fact, about one-third of all students will swap institutions at least once before earning their degree.

> Transferring colleges can be a great move if you're sure that the new school offers opportunities your current school lacks.

Transferring colleges can be a great move if you're sure that the new school offers opportunities your current school lacks. That said, transferring involves an application process, and competition for open spots can be fierce, especially at prestigious and highly-selective schools.

First, let's look at why some students decide to transfer.

1.) **They're unhappy.** One excellent reason to transfer is because you are unhappy. If you find that the school you are attending is not the best-fit college for you, you don't have to settle for four years of misery. Now that you have more clarity about what you want out of your college experience, you are even better equipped to find one that will meet your academic and social expectations.

2.) **They want to pursue an academic or career interest that's not supported at their current school.** Another reason to transfer is if your current school does not have a strong program in your major or area of interest. If you've decided to be a doctor and your college has a weak pre-med program, don't be afraid to look elsewhere.

3.) **They want another shot at their first-choice college.** Some students who are rejected from their first-choice school attend another school with the intention of later transferring. Others begin their education at a two-year community college but ultimately want a four-year degree.

4.) **They want to save tuition dollars.** A student might decide to enroll at a less expensive school close to home so they can save money, and then transfer to a more expensive school after one or two years. This strategy can save families thousands of dollars and make a financial reach school more affordable.

I will say that if your goal is simply to enroll in a college with bigger name recognition, you might want to reconsider. The difference in reputation between your old school and your new one may not justify the time and effort of transferring.

Transfer Applications

If you do end up deciding to transfer colleges, you'll fill out another college application (this time it might be a designated Transfer Student Application or the Common App for transfer application, depending on the school). That's right—you'll collect letters of recommendation, submit test scores, and write another round of essays.

There are some key differences though from applying to colleges the first time around.

- For one thing, your high school transcript and test scores will take a back seat to your college transcript. Standardized test scores are used (in theory) to predict college grades. Once you have college grades, the scores are less important. So, earn strong grades in college if you hope to transfer (some schools will still want to see your SAT or ACT scores as well).

- Colleges have different policies for transfer students but typically expect you to have acquired a minimum number of credits. You'll have a harder time transferring if you've completed more than two years of study, even if you abandon some of the credit you've accrued.

- Colleges usually expect transfer applicants to have clear, compelling academic reasons for wanting to switch schools. The best reason is a strong desire to pursue a course of study or experience that isn't offered at your present school. You'll have to make your case in detail and be convincing. A transfer applicant, unlike a first-year applicant, can't get away with being "undecided" about academic or career goals.

- Of course, transferring can impact your intended graduation date or study abroad plans. Be aware of the policies at your prospective transfer school. Not all classes/credits are transferable, and some schools won't accept credit from a class if you earned below a C.

Financial Considerations

Typically, transfer students are eligible for less scholarship funds than first-year students, though some schools set aside money specifically for transfer students. If you go this route, be sure to ask your prospective schools about their financial aid policies. You'll want to make sure your transfer college is a great financial fit!

Transfer Acceptance Rates

Okay, back to the original question. How difficult is it to transfer? According to NACAC's 2017 *State of College Admission* report[2], the transfer acceptance rate is slightly lower than the freshman acceptance rate: "Among institutions that enroll transfer students, average selectivity for Fall 2016 was 62 percent, compared to 66 percent for first-time freshmen." Of course, your odds of acceptance as a transfer student can differ on a school-by-school basis, as you can see in the chart on the next page. It's often significantly more difficult to be accepted to a selective school as a transfer student than it is right out of high school. Duke University, for example, accepted around 11 percent of freshman applicants for academic year 2016-2017 but only 3 percent of transfer applicants.

School	# of applicants	% applicants accepted	# of transfer applicants	% transfer applicants accepted
Stanford University	43,997	5%	1,959	2%
Harvard College	39,041	5%	1,491	1%
Massachusetts Institute of Technology	19,020	8%	569	5%
Duke University	31,671	11%	1,985	3%
New York University	60,724	32%	7,318	24%
University of Michigan— Ann Arbor	55,503	29%	3,988	39%

*Data reported to The Princeton Review by the school in spring 2016

To boost your chances, keep those grades up, and use some old-fashioned interpersonal methods: contact college admission officers directly, and keep in touch with them.

2 https://www.nacacnet.org/news--publications/publications/state-of-college-admission/

I want to take a gap year (year off between high school and college). How will that impact my chances of admission?

If you are interested in taking a year "off" between high school and college, I recommend applying to college as a high school senior and deferring your acceptance once you get in. The same applies if you anticipate you may need to take a semester or year off before beginning college due to family or health issues. Deferred acceptance is available at most colleges (although if you're applying Early Decision or taking advantage of any immediate-decision admission offers, I recommend you confirm that deferral is allowed under those circumstances). Completing your college application while you're still in school, on a regular schedule, and in touch with your teachers, administrators, and high school counselors will be infinitely easier than pulling all of that together after graduation. Plus, knowing where you'll be in a few months or a year will give you peace of mind and allow you to make the most of your semester or year away from school.

Most colleges support students who are interested in taking gap years to travel, work, or serve a community. There is a wide variety of internship, fellowship, and travel programs targeting people in between high school and college. Many require fees or travel costs; some are structured to be cost-neutral; and some offer pay. If time off is necessary to address your health or your family, most colleges and universities are willing to work with you to form a path to graduation.

After you receive your acceptance letter, talk to your college, and see if they'll let you start a semester or year later than you had originally planned. Find out what your college needs from you in order to consider your deferment request. Most schools require a formal letter including a description of what you plan to do with your time away from school, and, occasionally, a deposit to save your spot. And as with most college-related activities, there will be a deadline. Find out what it is before you try to delay your enrollment.

Keep in mind: Even if you've already applied for financial aid your senior year, you will need to re-apply by completing the FAFSA before you return to school after your gap year. Be sure to ask your college about its financial aid policies for deferred enrollment students.

Some colleges and universities even offer the chance to spend your first semester abroad (or in an environment outside the classroom), giving you a built-in gap semester. There are several colleges that offer gap year programs for admitted students. Princeton University, for example, offers a tuition-free Bridge Year Program, which facilitates nine months of international community service for select admitted students. Tufts University and University of North Carolina at Chapel Hill have similar fellowship programs that offer funded service years to admitted students.

The bottom line? If you have a clear sense of what you want to do with your gap year, and a concrete opportunity to pursue it, you'll arrive on campus with even more to offer than you have as a college senior. If you want to take a year off simply because you think a break might be nice after twelve years of school, I suggest you buckle down and head off to college right away. Depending on learning styles and thinking patterns, it can be very difficult for some students to re-enter the structure and schedule of university life after a year away. A college degree is too valuable to risk derailing it for an early taste of the "real world."

How can a parent participate most effectively in their child's college application process?

I love this question. Parents, I know the college admission process can be a stressful one for you, too.

Family members can be the biggest cheerleaders for the kids in their life going through the process, but often don't know *how or how much* to be involved.

Sometimes parents hold back because they feel shaky themselves on the admission process or feel that applying to college is an important rite of passage that students should do all on their own.

Other parents feel their best role is to act as hand-holder or drill sergeant, putting their kids through their college application paces.

> Family members can be a huge support to the students in their life by offering both moral and logistical support.

Folks, there is a happy medium! Parents and other family members can be a huge support to the students in their life by offering both moral and logistical support in tackling that long list of college application tasks. Build up morale by offering to take your child on college tours and to visit college fairs. Help them research and compare colleges. Ask lots of questions!

When it comes to college conversations, my six biggest tips are:

1. **Set some ground rules.** This might seem like a no brainer, but it's extremely important for parents to get their own college worries in check before broaching these weighty topics with students. You want conversations with your child to be positive and productive. Don't pass your stress along to your students because they may not want to open up to you later when they hit an application snag. Your kids are going to take their cues from you about how to approach the college admission process. Remember you're on stage all the time. You don't have to be perfect, but when you sense yourself losing your perspective, revert back to setting good examples.

2. **Start early.** This is the MOST popular piece of advice given by parents who have gone through the process. (About 50 percent of respondents to our annual Colleges Hopes & Worries Survey say this). Refer back to Chapter 3 where I outline exactly what students should be doing in 9th, 10th, 11th, and 12th grades to prepare for the college admission process. I've said it before folks, but planning ahead won't just set your child up to succeed, it will actually make the process so much less stressful. (More about stress later!)

3. **Help students find balance.** It's possible to be too focused on getting into college. Of course, we all want our children and students to care about their futures. But if they make every decision in high school based on how it will look to colleges, they're trying to game the system rather than follow their own interests. That never works in college admissions, and it doesn't make for a happy, confident kid, either. So, don't tie everything students do to college. Help them separate and find a balance between college planning and the other parts of their lives. They'll be more content and more successful college applicants if you do. (Pro tip: Implement a "college-free" talk zone at the dinner table or on the ride home from school so your kids can get a break from college overload!)

4. **Create a rock-solid support system.** There's a reason you don't ask your doctor to do your taxes or your accountant to diagnose your knee pain. Go to the right sources. Your child's high school counselor, colleges' websites, college guidebooks, admission officers, representatives at college fairs, and students who attend the schools are good sources.

5. **Help your child figure out the kind of college atmosphere in which they'll thrive academically, personally, socially, and, yes, financially.** This all goes back to "best fit colleges," which I discuss back in Chapter 1. It's not all about where your child can get in, where you, the parent, went to college, or the college with the best name recognition. You're looking for the schools that will fit your student to a T. You know your child best (and probably feel you know best about where they would thrive), but be patient with your child as they work through the journey. Communicate your opinions but be open to negotiating with your student and to compromise. That being said, do talk about finances and college costs early on, and make sure a financial safety school (one your child would be thrilled to attend) makes it on their list.

6. **Ask your student: "What's the best way for me to help you?"** Parents who deliver meticulously organized file folders with college lists and typed up college essays to their teen's door are likely to be met with more than a few eye rolls. (It goes without saying that parents should NEVER write their child's essays or fill out their applications for them). Let your child take the reins on certain pieces of the process and slowly gain more and more responsibility. This is the first major project your child is going to undertake with no final grade and no teacher leading the way! Your role is to help them strategize and divide and conquer.

That's my advice for parents. But what about for students? Lean on your parents when you need to, but don't let them make all the decisions!

Parent to Parent: 8 Tips Parents of College-Bound Students Need to Know

1. "Listen to your child!—Maureen, Middletown, NY

2. "Allow your child to dream about anything he can be!" — Susan, Remsenburg, NJ

3. "Be a guide and not a choice-maker. Believe in your child's own intuitions and advocate for their personal interests." — Alice, Randolph, NJ

4. "As a parent, allow your kid to experience the college application for themselves. While it is imperative to gently look over their shoulders, taking over full control doesn't allow them to make important decisions for themselves." — Danielle, Lambertville, NJ

5. "Be encouraging but not micromanaging. Remind your child of upcoming deadlines and help them proofread their essays. Start early in researching colleges that might be a good fit. Visit a bookstore and help your child pick out a good review manual for the ACT and/or SAT." — Carole, Livonia, MI

6. "I know some parents who are literally obsessing over this whole process. I hope they don't forget that it is their child that is going to college, not them." — Nancy, WI

7. "Focus on your child and what is best for him/her and try not to focus on all the competition between parents. This is about your child, not about you." — Carol, Tarrytown, NY

8. "Parents, Back off! Applicants, Relax!" — D.B., Monterey, CA

—2017 College Hopes & Worries Survey

How do I balance school work, extracurriculars, test prep, college applications, family, social life, and SANITY?!

In the words of one recent college applicant who completed our annual College Hopes & Worries Survey: "Whoever said that senior year is the easiest is a liar."

I do not envy the schedule of today's high school students one bit. Between homework, extracurriculars, and maintaining a social life, college-bound students are facing very serious pressures, not the least of which is the overwhelming terrain of the college admission process.

Just know that you are not alone. I hope that this book has done some good in diffusing the perceived enormity of the process. Now that you understand the timeline and have a sense of the steps you need to accomplish, take a deep breath and dig in.

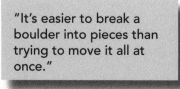

"It's easier to break a boulder into pieces than trying to move it all at once."

First, it's important to get organized. Make a college checklist of all the things you need to do for your applications. (We've got a great one in the Appendix.) From asking teachers for college recommendations to applying for financial aid and scholarships, assign yourself deadlines and put them all on the list. Then, plot your application-related deadlines in a notebook or calendar app along with your homework, projects, and papers. Don't forget to schedule time on the calendar for your away games or work shifts. The goal is to map out everything you must accomplish over the month, semester, or year.

Not only does this system ensure that nothing falls through the cracks, but plotting your schedule will help you see your pressure points. Do you have a college application deadline and a major chem final on the same day? Avoid a head-on collision by getting your application done early! Remember, you can't necessarily study too far in advance, but you can work on your applications whenever you have some down time—like drafting those college essays over Spring or Summer break.

Ok, you've laid out all your to-dos in a big old grid/worksheet/calendar. Now what? Take things one step at a time. Break your big projects into little ones. It's easier to plan, and every task you get done will help you feel more confident and accomplished. As one college counselor I know puts it, "It's easier to break a boulder into pieces than trying to move it all at once."

Remember: You have a support system. Your friends, your parents, and your college counselors are all in your corner. Just talking with others can be a source of help, as well to relieve some of the stress of becoming too wrapped up in your own situation. Take advantage of workshops your guidance office may offer on specific aspects of the admission process. At The Princeton Review, we offer quite a few free webinars on many college admission topics. (Check them out at PrincetonReview.com/webinars.)

The bottom line on stress? Though there isn't much that students can do to get the colleges to send out those big and little envelopes any faster, there are some strategies to prevent the worst stress. If you ask lots of questions to help you understand the process, start early, take it one step at a time, and apply to several carefully selected, appropriate schools, you can rest assured that you've done everything in your power to make the process go as smoothly as possible.

5 Things a College Counselor Can Do for You

1. **Lower your college stress.** Applications are stressful, but knowing that there are college experts on your side can make all the difference.

2. **Make a college wishlist.** Talking to your counselor about your dreams and what's important to you in academics, campus life, and financial aid will help you figure out what you really want out of college.

3. **Find and compare colleges.** College counselors are pros at helping you research the schools that are the right fit to your unique personality and goals.

4. **Help you rise to the top.** Your college counselor will help you position the rest of your application to tell your story through your essays, extracurricular activities, and letters of recommendation.

5. **Choose the right school for you.** Your counselor will help you craft your list of dream, match and safety schools and create the right application strategy for your college wishlist.

Appendix

College Bound: Your Admission Checklist

What's the trick to less college admission stress? Start early, and take small steps along the way.

Freshman Year

☐ Focus on your grades so you can earn placement for more rigorous courses.

☐ Practice your study skills, identify support resources available, and ask for help if you need it.

☐ Get to know your school and community! Explore clubs, sports, volunteer opportunities, and more.

☐ Take any appropriate SAT Subject Tests.

Sophomore Year

☐ Continue to challenge yourself academically.

☐ Develop constructive relationships with your teachers.

☐ Get to know your school counselor.

☐ Commit to the activities that you really enjoy, and try to take on more responsibility.

☐ Take any appropriate SAT Subject Tests.

Summer Before Junior Year

☐ This is the perfect time to prep for the SAT and ACT.

☐ Begin your college research.

Junior Year

☐ Take the SAT and ACT when you're ready.

☐ Balance schoolwork and outside-school interests.

☐ Take the most challenging courses available to you.

☐ Take the PSAT/NMSQT in October to qualify for a National Merit Scholarship and other scholarship opportunities.

☐ Start gathering teacher recommendations.

☐ Narrow your college list and try to visit one or two campuses while class is in session.

☐ Make a plan to prepare for AP exams in May and SAT Subject Tests in June.

☐ Learn about financial aid and available scholarships.

Summer Before Senior Year

☐ Start working on your application and prewriting college essays—they take longer than you think!

☐ Make a calendar of all your application deadlines so you can stay on track.

☐ If possible, consider visiting colleges that have made it to the top of your target list.

☐ If you are applying for Early Decision, you should take the SAT or ACT no later than September.

Senior Fall

☐ Apply early if you're a strong candidate.

☐ Wrap up your applications and stay on top of deadlines for apps, scholarships, and financial aid.

☐ Don't get senioritis! Senior grades matter—your first term grades will definitely be used in the admission process.

☐ Complete your last SAT/ACT by December at the latest.

Senior Spring

☐ If you still have AP exams to take, study!

☐ Send thank-you notes to your recommenders.

☐ Get ready to celebrate! Spring is all about acceptance letters rolling in.

☐ Talk to friends, family, and counselors before making your final choice.

☐ Once you decide, don't look back! Read through your college's course catalog, and look forward to the next four years.

Here's Another Helpful Book

In The Princeton Review's *The Complete Book of Colleges* you'll find meticulously researched information that will help you narrow the search for the best college for you. Each of the 1,355 user-friendly profiles answers your questions, including about tuition and other costs, average test scores, popular majors, student housing, and key campus organizations.

Find out more about kicking off your college search in Chapter 1.

High School Testing Timeline

Extracurricular activities, school commitments, and other factors place into when and how you're going to prepare for the SAT and ACT.

If you're taking both tests, you need to leave enough time to take each test twice. It's ideal for students to prep for the SAT over the summer and take the PSAT in October. You'll be ready for the PSAT because you will have already prepared for the SAT.

Folks, there's no perfect plan. Here's what I recommend for students going into their junior year.

Prep for the SAT and ACT, AP Exams, and SAT Subject Tests

☐ **Summer before junior year:** Prep for the SAT and take it in August or October for the first time.

☐ **October:** Take the PSAT.

☐ **November/December:** Take the SAT one more time.

☐ **February:** Start prepping for the ACT and take it for the first time.

☐ **April:** Take the ACT one more time.

☐ **May:** Study, and take your AP tests.

☐ **June:** Sign up for one to three SAT Subject Tests.

☐ **Summer before senior year:** You can take the SAT or ACT one more time if necessary. If you take a summer test, you receive scores in time for Early Action or Early Decision deadlines.

20 Financial Aid Terms You Need To Know

1. **Financial Aid.** A general term used to refer to a variety of programs funded by the federal and state governments as well as the individual schools to assist students with their educational costs. While the names may vary, financial aid comes in three basic forms: (1) gift aid (grants and scholarships) that does not have to be paid back (2) student loans, and (3) work-study jobs.

2. **Cost of Attendance:** A figure, estimated by the school, that includes the cost of tuition, fees, room, board, books, and supplies as well as an allowance for transportation and personal expenses. This figure is compared to the Expected Family Contribution to determine a student's aid eligibility.

3. **Expected Family Contribution (EFC):** The amount of money the family is expected to contribute for the year toward the student's cost of attendance. This figure is compared to the Cost of Attendance to determine a student's aid eligibility.

4. **Parent's Contribution:** The amount of money the parent(s) are expected to contribute for the year toward the student's Cost of Attendance.

5. **Student's Contribution:** The amount of money the student is expected to contribute for the year toward his or her cost of attendance.

6. **Need:** The amount of aid a student is eligible to receive. This figure is calculated by subtracting the Expected Family Contribution from the Cost of Attendance.

7. **Need Analysis Forms:** Aid applications used to calculate the expected family contribution. The most common need analysis forms are: the Free Application for Federal Student Aid (FAFSA) and the CSS/Financial Aid PROFILE form. Consult the individual school's financial aid filing requirements to determine which form(s) are required for that particular school.

8. **Free Application for Federal Student Aid (FAFSA):** The need analysis document written by the U.S. Department of Education. This form is required for virtually all students seeking financial aid including the unsubsidized Stafford loan.

9. **Student Aid Report (SAR):** The multi-page report that is issued to students who have filed a completed FAFSA.

10. **CSS/Financial Aid PROFILE:** A need analysis application created and processed by the College Board. Also known as the CSS PROFILE or the PROFILE form.

11. **Institutional Forms:** Supplemental forms required by the individual schools to determine aid eligibility.

12. **Gift Aid:** Financial aid, usually a grant or scholarship, that does not have to be paid back and that does not involve employment.

13. **Grants:** Gift aid that is generally based on need. The programs can be funded by the federal and state governments as well as the individual schools.

14. **Pell Grant:** A federally funded need-based grant program for first-time undergraduate students (i.e., the student has not as yet earned a bachelor's or first professional degree). Funds from this program are generally awarded to lower- and lower-middle-income families. Years ago, this program was called the Basic Educational Opportunity Grant (BEOG).

15. **Scholarships:** Gift aid that is usually based on merit or a combination of need and merit.

16. **Self-Help:** The portion of the aid package relating to student loans and/or work-study.

17. **Direct Loan Program:** Formerly known as the Stafford Student Loan program, this federally funded program provides low-interest loans to undergraduate and graduate students. In most cases, repayment does not begin until six months after the student graduates or leaves school and there are no interest charges while the student is in school. For new loans disbursed after June 30, 2006, the interest rate is fixed. (Prior loans had variable rates.) There are two types of Direct loans: subsidized and unsubsidized. The subsidized Direct loan is need-based and the government pays the interest while the student is in school. The unsubsidized Direct loan is non-need-based and can be taken out by virtually all students. In many cases, students can elect to let the interest accumulate until after they graduate.

18. **Parents Loans for Undergraduate Students (PLUS):** A federally sponsored educational loan program in which parents can borrow up to the total cost of attendance minus any financial aid received for each child in an undergraduate program. Eligibility is not based on need.

19. **Perkins Loan Program:** This federally funded need-based program provides low interest loans to undergraduate and graduate students and is administered by the school's financial aid office. In most cases, repayment does not begin until nine months after the student graduates or leaves school and there are no interest charges while the student is in school. The fixed interest rate is currently 5 percent.

20. **Federal Work Study (FWS):** A federally funded aid program that provides jobs for students. Eligibility is based on need.

Here's Another Helpful Book

My book *Colleges That Create Futures: 50 Schools That Launch Careers By Going Beyond the Classroom* salutes an extraordinary group of institutions with compelling commitments to helping students segue to successful careers and post-graduate accomplishments.

Check out a sampling of noteworthy campus experiences in Chapter 1.

26 Tips for Getting Financial Aid, Scholarships, and Grants and for Paying Less for College

When it comes to actually paying for college, there is a lot of information out there. A great resource is our annual book *Paying for College Without Going Broke* by my friend Kalman Chany. Here, I present some tips from Kal for applying for financial aid and trimming the costs of college.

Getting Financial Aid

1. **Learn how financial aid works.** The more and the sooner you know about how need-based aid eligibility is determined, the better you can take steps to maximize such eligibility.

2. **Apply for financial aid no matter what your circumstances.** Some merit-based aid can only be awarded if the applicant has submitted financial aid application forms.

3. **Don't wait until the student is accepted to apply for financial aid.** Do it when applying for admission.

4. **Complete all the required aid applications.** All students seeking aid must submit the FAFSA (Free Application for Federal Student Aid); other forms may also be required. Check with each college to see what's required and when.

5. **Get the best scores you can on the SAT or ACT.** They are used not only in decisions for admission but they can also impact financial aid. If your scores and other stats exceed the school's admission criteria, you are likely to get a better aid package than a marginal applicant.

6. **Apply strategically to colleges.** Your chances of getting aid will be better at schools that have generous financial aid budgets. (Check the Financial Aid Ratings for various schools on PrincetonReview.com.)

7. **Don't rule out any school as too expensive.** A generous aid award from a pricey private school can make it less costly than a public school with a lower sticker price.

8. **Take advantage of education tax benefits.** A dollar saved on taxes is worth the same as a dollar in scholarship aid. Look into Coverdells, 529 Plans, education tax credits, and loan deductions.

Scholarships and Grants

9. **Get your best possible score on the PSAT:** It is the National Merit Scholarship Qualifying Test and also used in the selection of students for other scholarships and recognition programs.

10. **Check your eligibility for grants and scholarships from your state.** Some (but not all) states will allow you to use such funds out of state.

11. **Look for scholarships locally.** Find out if your employer offers scholarships or tuition assistance plans for employees or family members. Also look into scholarships from your community groups and high school, as well as your church, temple, or mosque.

12. **Look for outside scholarships realistically:** they account for less than five percent of aid awarded. Research them at PrincetonReview.com or other free sites. Steer clear of scholarship search firms that charge fees and "promise" scholarships.

Paying for College

13. **Start saving early when the student is an infant.** Too late? Start now. The more you save, the less you'll have to borrow.

14. **Invest wisely.** Considering a 529 plan? Compare your own state's plan which may have tax benefits with other states' programs. Get info at savingforcollege.com.

15. **If you have to borrow, first pursue federal education loans (Direct or PLUS).** Avoid private loans at all costs.

16. **Never put tuition on a credit card.** The debt is more expensive than ever given recent changes to interest rates and other fees some card issuers are now charging.

17. **Try not to take money from a retirement account or 401(k) to pay for college.** In addition to likely early distribution penalties and additional income taxes, the higher income will reduce your aid eligibility.

Paying Less for College

18. **Attend a community college for two years and transfer to a pricier school to complete the degree.** Plan ahead: Be sure the college you plan to transfer to will accept the community college credits.

19. **Look into "cooperative education" programs.** Over 900 colleges allow students to combine college education with a job. It can take longer to complete a degree this way. But graduates generally owe less in student loans and have a better chance of getting hired.

20. **Take as many AP courses as possible and get high scores on AP exams.** Many colleges award course credits for high AP scores. Some students have cut a year off their college tuition this way.

21. **Earn college credit via "dual enrollment" programs available at some high schools.** These allow students to take college level courses during their senior year.

22. **Earn college credits by taking CLEP (College-Level Examination Program) exams.** Depending on the college, a qualifying score on any of the thirty-three CLEP exams can earn students three to twelve college credits. (See Princeton Review's *Cracking the CLEP*, 5th Edition.)

23. **Stick to your college and your major.** Changing colleges can result in lost credits. Aid may be limited/not available for transfer students at some schools. Changing majors can mean paying for extra courses to meet requirements.

24. **Finish college in three years if possible.** Take the maximum number of credits every semester, attend summer sessions, and earn credits via online courses. Some colleges offer three-year programs for high-achieving students.

25. **Let Uncle Sam pay for your degree.** ROTC (Reserve Officer Training Corps) programs available from U.S. Armed Forces branches (except the Coast Guard) offer merit-based scholarships up to full tuition via participating colleges in exchange for military service after you graduate.

26. **Better yet:** Attend a tuition-free college.

Please visit PrincetonReview.com/college-advice for the most up-to-date information on available financial aid programs.

2017 College Hopes & Worries Survey Results

Every year, we survey college applicants and their parents about their perspective on the admission process. We ask about their dream schools, their biggest challenges, and what factors into their search for the schools that will fit them best. Check out some of our key findings! You can find the most recent survey results on PrincetonReview.com/college-hopes-worries.

Findings for our 2017 survey are based on responses from 10,519 people: 8,499 college applicants and 2,020 parents of college applicants. They came from all fifty states and Washington D.C., plus more than twenty countries abroad.

Top 10 Dream Schools

Student's Picks

1. Stanford University

2. Harvard College

3. Massachusetts Institute of Technology

4. New York University

5. University of California—Los Angeles

6. Columbia University

7. Princeton University

8. University of California—Berkeley

9. University of Pennsylvania

10. Yale University

Parent's Picks

1. Stanford University

2. Princeton University

3. Harvard College

4. Massachusetts Institute of Technology

5. Duke University

6. University of Pennsylvania

7. University of Michigan—Ann Arbor

8. New York University

9. Cornell University

10. University of Notre Dame

The College Process

How many colleges do students apply to?

42% said they/their child would apply to 5 to 8 colleges

30% said they/their child would apply to 9 or more colleges

What is the toughest part of the college admission process?

37%: Taking SAT, ACT, or AP exams

33%: Completing applications for admission and financial aid

21%: Waiting for the decision letters/choosing which college to attend

9%: Researching colleges/choosing schools to apply to

Biggest College Worries

College Costs

85% estimated their college cost will be more than $50,000 (Within that cohort 43% estimated it to be more than $100,000)

61% of parents estimated the costs as more than $100,000

39% of students estimated the costs as more than $100,000

Biggest Worry? Debt

Biggest worry in 2006: Won't get into top choice college. (In 2006, the biggest concern among the majority (34%) was... "Won't get into first-choice college.")

Biggest worry in 2007-2012: Won't afford their top choice (From 2007 to 2012), the biggest concern among the majority (34%) was... "Will get into their first-choice college but won't have sufficient funds/aid to attend it.")

Biggest worry in 2013-2017: Level of debt (Debt has been the biggest concern among respondents (parents and students alike) for the past three years. The majority (38%) said... "Level of debt...to pay for the degree.")

Greatest College Hopes

Choosing a college

9%: College with best academic reputation

8%: College that will be the most affordable

41%: Choose a college with best program for my (my child's) career interests

42%: Choose a college that will be the best overall fit

Benefit of a College Degree

26%: The education

32%: The exposure to new ideas

42%: The potentially better job and higher income

More Advice from the Experts: Smart Tips from College-Bound Students for Next Year's Applicants

Every year on our College Hopes & Worries Survey, we include an optional question at the end that asks respondents what advice they have for next year's applicants and parents of applicants. Here, in their own words, are the suggestions and tips of our respondents. Enjoy!

On the College Application Process

"Start early. As a matter of fact, start now."

"Two Words: Start Early! Deadlines creep up quicker than you may anticipate. In addition, there are little things that you need to do to fulfill the application requirements. By starting early you can reduce stress levels and assure that you have enough time to get everything finished without rushing."

"Research, research, research. The better educated you are about the colleges, the better chance you will get the education you really want."

"Be excited to write your college application essays. They WILL definitely be tough, but in the end, you'll look back at the experience and smile because you learn so much about yourself as a human being. It's actually quite a wonderful experience, but only if you're willing to make it a wonderful experience."

"Make sure that you apply or consider all the schools that you could possibly conceive yourself going to. Nothing is worse than 'February syndrome' in which you realize you didn't apply to a school that you could see yourself attending."

On Stress

"College is about finding your happiness, not your parents' happiness or what would look good on your bumper. Be open-minded."

"Don't get frustrated with applications. Just think of how good you'll feel in the fall walking the halls of your chosen college."

"Have fun with it! If you enjoy the process along the way, the outcome will hopefully be more beneficial."

"Do not get too nervous. It's not always about getting into the most known school."

"Don't worry! It's going to be okay."

On College Visits

"Visit! The feel of a school is entirely important. I visited what I thought would be my top school and campus didn't feel like home. On the other hand, I visited a college I didn't think I would be interested in and it just felt right."

"Visit as many colleges as possible and talk to students in college asking what you like the most and least about their college."

"Visit every college you can! Get interviews, tours, info sessions, overnights, and attend classes."

"The visit (even if during the summer) is the most important part. It gave me an idea of what it would be like to live there. I saw the location, toured the buildings and met administrators. I ended up choosing a college I never imagined I would like over ones I had dreamed about for years."

"Visit schools sooner and spend an entire day/overnight to get a feel for what will be offered to us to help us get ready for the world. Sitting in on classes that would be part of my major would also give me an indication of what is expected of me so I could be a better student."

On Money Matters

"Don't let the cost of a college scare you. Apply anyways because financial aid is always available."

"Money is a huge factor for both you and your child. It is extremely important that you give your child a 'budget' for your peace of mind and theirs."

"Scholarships! Make sure you apply for as many scholarships as possible."

"Don't give up, apply to your dream school even if you can't afford it, you might be surprised by how much financial aid is offered."

"More expensive colleges are not always better colleges."

On Rejection

"When you think you didn't get into the school you wanted, you might be getting into the school you needed."

"You are smart. Don't let a rejection letter make you feel depressed."

"There is a place for everyone. Relax and think of it as a journey—not a race to be won, but a home to be found."

"It's not as bad as everyone makes it out to be. Don't worry so much about where you're going. Worry more about the mindset you go to school with."

"Try not to stress too much about the possibility of not being accepted into your first-choice college, because you'll go half mad if you do so."

On Choosing Which College to Attend

"Don't worry so much about what other people think is the best college for you. The only opinion that matters is your own because you will be the one spending four years of your life there. Pick the college you feel most comfortable at."

"Learn as much as you can about the college application process. Things have changed so much from the time my parents went through this."

"Don't rule out schools just because they aren't Ivy League caliber. Smaller schools have a lot to offer."

"Don't be afraid of traveling far from home and don't go somewhere just because friends are going there."

"Don't focus on your first choice. Widen your eyes to keep your options open."

Parent to Parent: What I Wish I'd Known

Every year on our College Hopes & Worries Survey, we include an optional question at the end that asks respondents what advice they have for next year's applicants and parents of applicants. Here's what the parents had to say.

On the College Application Process

"Start sooner!" — Linda, Tampa FL

"Start early, and save early for their future." — Loreli, Chandler, AZ

"Start Early! Visit schools in sophomore year, concentrate on testing in junior year, apply in senior year. " — Karen, Woodinville, WA

"Start preparing in your child's first year of high school . Don't wait until third year. " — Carlene, Roseville, CA

"Start the whole process a year earlier than you think you need to." — Amy, Glen Ellyn, IL

"When thinking about which schools to consider, our daughter seemed stuck because she isn't sure what she wants to be. We tried to help her just think about three to five things she likes and would want to learn more about. That seemed to help take off the pressure and get her 'unstuck' with choosing some schools to visit." — Ellen, New Paltz, NY

"Create a calendar with deadlines, test dates , college events and visits, etc. This will eliminate a lot of stress for you and your child." — Sandee, Los Gatos, CA

"Treat the application process like a job. Set a regular time each week to tackle some aspect of the process." — Laura, ME

"After your child applies, the schools will allow you access to their website to track your application information. Keep track of all of your child's passwords and website access information. Because schools use different safety systems, you can end up with different user IDs and passwords at each school. If you apply to more than three schools, this can be quite confusing." — Cheryl, Stevenson Ranch, CA

"Do what you can to make sure your child 'owns' the entire application process. Start the FAFSA and CSS early as they require a lot of information and pay careful attention to the instructions. Don't wait until the last day to apply for anything as the servers frequently get overloaded." — James, CA

On Stress

"Relax! Somehow, it all comes together. Everyone goes through it, so ask your family and friends for advice/help. You will be surprised at the great advice you can gather that way." — Sharon, Brielle, NJ

"Your child will not be nearly as stressed as you will be." — Lynda, Sunrise, FL

"Don't spend too much time comparing notes with others going through the process. Makes people crazy." — Sarah, Newton, MA

"Try not to stress too much—enjoy the process and make the most of the time you spend with your child, talking about his/her interests, helping them take that big step." — Sharon, Amherst, MA

"Make sure to take the college process in steps and you won't feel so overwhelmed." — Denise, Sea Girt, NJ

On College Visits

"Visit as many schools as you can. A visit can change your view of a school." — Jeanne, IN

"When visiting colleges, don't just take the packaged tour. Eat in the dining halls and talk with the students." — John, Orange, CT

"Visit colleges when they are in session." — Mariko, Jamaica, NY

"Do college visits with your child and make it a fun experience. Spend a night if you can in the city you are going to to get a feel of the surroundings. Also, it is fun to experience the excitement of your child when they have decided on a college! The special family time is never going to be the same, so cherish this important decision on the right college." — Katlin, Olathe, KS

"Visit the school more than once and take pictures because when you visit it all becomes a blur. "— Lucy, NY

On Parenting

"Listen to your child!" — Maureen, Middletown, NY

"Allow your child to dream about anything he can be!" —Susan, Remsenburg, NJ

"Be a guide and not a choice-maker. Believe in your child's own intuitions and advocate for their personal interests." — Alice, Randolph, NJ

"As a parent, allow your kid to experience the college application for themselves. While it is imperative to gently look over their shoulders, taking over full control doesn't allow them to make important decisions for themselves." — Danielle, Lambertville, NJ

"I know some parents who are literally obsessing over this whole process. I hope they don't forget that it is their child that is going to college, not them." — Nancy, WI

On Money Matters

"Look at the average financial aid package, not just cost, and don't say no to yourself (your child) on behalf of a school by never applying to it." — Charles, Philadelphia, PA

"Dare to dream. Don't limit your child's vision of their future by your own financial worries." — Karen, VA

"Don't be scared off from applying to private schools as opposed to public universities. Private schools can be very generous with scholarship offers." — Diane, Chicago IL

"Let your child free to see what schools will accept your child and see what the financials are later. In other words, do not assume a school is too much money as a reason not to apply. Particularly if your child has done well on ACT/SAT, the tuition number at a private school is not going to be the number you will have to fund." — Alan, MI

"Do your homework on the entire process, including understanding how the financial aid process works, and don't wait until the last minute to delve into this stuff. " — Ken, Colorado Springs, CO

On Choosing Which College to Attend

"Let your student take the lead in defining interests and schools that could be a good fit. Don't focus on labels. An excellent education can be had in schools you've never heard about before." — C.L., Ridgewood, NJ

"Don't be overly focused on 'brand name' colleges. There are other excellent choices that offer very good value, and are quite affordable." — Mark, Macungie, PA

"Don't focus on a major so much as interests and opportunities. Nobody is sure at 18 what they want to do. The beauty of college is you have a chance to expand your horizons and perspective." — Larry, Bayside, NY

"There are many good colleges out there—not just the ten that everyone is applying to." — M.M., Far Hills, NJ

"Make the final decision after receiving all the financial aid packages." — Kathleen, FL

Here's Another Helpful Book

The K&W Guide to Colleges for Students with Learning Differences profiles over 350 schools highly recommended for such students. It includes strategies to help them successfully apply to the best programs for their needs, plus advice from learning specialists on making an effective transition to college.

Index

B

C

D

I

J

L

M

N

P

R

T

V

W

About the Author

Rob Franek, Editor-in-Chief at The Princeton Review is the company's main authority on higher education and a college aficionado: he visits more than 50 colleges a year. Over his 24-year career in education, he has served as a college admissions administrator, test prep teacher, author, and lecturer. He is lead author of The Princeton Review's annual books, *The Best 382 Colleges*, and *Colleges That Pay You Back: The 200 Schools That Give You the Best Bang for Your Tuition Buck*. He is also author of *Colleges That Create Futures: 50 Schools That Launch Careers by Going Beyond the Classroom* and co-author of *If The U Fits: Expert Advice on Finding the Right College and Getting Accepted*. Rob gives dozens of presentations a year to audiences of teachers, parents, and students on trending education and college topics. Follow his Tweets at @RobFranek.

Notes

Notes

Notes